THE BOOK OF THE LOVER AND THE BELOVED

The traditional iconographic image of Ramon Llull, from an edition of his *Apostrophe* printed by Pere Posa at Barcelona in 1504.

Ramon Llull

THE BOOK OF THE LOVER AND THE BELOVED

An English Translation with Latin and Old Catalan
Versions Transcribed from Original Manuscripts

by

Mark D. Johnston

Foreword by Geoffrey Pridham

Aris & Phillips Ltd – Warminster – England
in association with
The Centre for Mediterranean Studies,
University of Bristol

ISBN 0 85668 633 6 (cloth)
ISBN 0 85668 634 4 (limp)

British Library Cataloguing-in-Publication Data
A catalogue record for this book is available from the British Library.

Published in association with
The Centre for Mediterranean Studies, University of Bristol.
Director: Geoffrey Pridham
and the Institut Català d'Estudis Mediterranis, Barcelona

The publishers gratefully acknowledge the financial assistance of the Institució de les Lletres Catalanes with this translation.

Printed and published in England by Aris & Phillips Ltd,
Teddington House, Warminster, Wilts. BA12 8PQ

Contents

Illustrations

Foreword

The publication of English-language translations of Catalan writers has for several years been one of the special programmes of the Centre for Mediterranean Studies (CMS) at Bristol University. It was felt that Catalan literature, not so widely known in Britain, had much to offer, given an increasing interest in works from Latin countries. The idea for this programme originated from the Centre's links with Barcelona, and owed some inspiration to the late Antoni Turull, who taught in Bristol University's Department of Hispanic, Portuguese and Latin American Studies until his death in 1990.

The CMS was established in 1987 as an interdisciplinary research centre, focussing its work on the socio-economic, political, cultural and historical problems of the countries of Mediterranean Europe, with a particular emphasis on modern and contemporary issues. It acts as a channel for collaborative work and for information and contacts between researchers in the field of Mediterranean Studies based in the UK and in other European countries, especially those in the Mediterranean region.

The CMS wishes to acknowledge the support of a maintenance grant from the European Commission in Brussels which has helped with furthering this programme of publishing Catalan writers in collaboration with Aris & Phillips. Two previous publications have appeared under this programme. A volume of short stories by Pere Calders, *The Virgin of the Railway and Other Stories*, translated by Amanda Bath, was published in 1991. Calders is one of the most important of contemporary Catalan writers, known primarily as a story-teller of humour and fantasy. The second result of this initiative to publish Catalan writers was the publication in 1994 of Joaquim Ruyra, *The Long Oar*, translated by Julie Flanagan. Ruyra lived and wrote somewhat earlier than Calders, his work being in the vanguard of the Modernist movement around the turn of the twentieth century.

The third publication is the present volume. *The Book of the Lover and the Beloved* by the Majorcan lay theologian and philosopher Ramon Llull (1232-1316) is an acknowledged classic of medieval mystical literature. His work is known both for its popular idiom and its combination of traditional Christian mystical imagery with an Islamic devotional spirit. The earlier translation by Allison Peers, published in 1926, is no longer available. A new translation can thus benefit from the availability now of full critical editions of Llull's original Old Catalan and Latin texts and research work in recent decades on Llull and on the language and ideas of Muslim mystical writers that influenced his work. A full introduction to the life and work of Llull has been written by Mark Johnston and is included in this volume.

Geoffrey Pridham, October 1995.

Matthaeo et Benjamin, a Deo datis

An engraving from the Latin edition of Llull's *Tree of Knowledge (Arbre de sciència)* printed at Barcelona by Pere Posa in 1505.

Introduction

The Career of Ramon Llull (1232-1316)

The *Book of the Lover and the Beloved* is the most celebrated work by one of the most unusual authors of the European Middle Ages. The details of Ramon Llull's biography are frustratingly obscure. Our chief source of knowledge about him is a very selective *Life* composed by his admirers at Paris in 1311; only a handful of other documents testify to the activities of his long career; his numerous writings include relatively few autobiographical references. This brief introduction cannot consider the many problematic aspects in Llull's life and work. It aims to give a summary of his achievements, as understood by this writer, for the benefit of general readers and non-specialist students of medieval history. Further details and discussion of Llull's career are available from the studies cited in this introduction (see especially the researches of Bonner and Hillgarth) and in the bibliography that follows.

Ramon Llull was born on Majorca, probably in 1232. He was the scion of a prosperous Catalan merchant family, which had helped to settle the island when king James I "The Conqueror" captured it from the Arabs in 1229. Llull evidently received the training in vernacular letters and courtesy typically given to well-born youths of this era. The *Life* opens by portraying him, around the age of 30, devoted to worldly pursuits, especially the composition of love lyrics. However, a series of powerful visions of Christ crucified moved him to abandon secular affairs and devote himself entirely to serving God. At this time, according to the *Life*, Llull conceived the three evangelical goals that became his life-long passion: writing "the best book in the world against the errors of the infidels"; promoting the creation of schools to train Christian missionaries in Oriental languages; and urging missions abroad among unbelievers. These objectives define both the context and the content for all his later work, including the *Book of the Lover and the Beloved*.

After confirming his vow with several pilgrimages, Llull devoted nearly a decade to private study and meditation on Majorca. He obtained a Moorish slave to teach him Arabic, and studied whatever texts of Islamic theology and philosophy he could obtain. The resources available on Majorca for advanced study of Islam were necessarily limited and probably somewhat old-fashioned (as suggested by Urvoy). He evidently did obtain compendia of doctrines from Algazel and perhaps similar popularizing summaries of other Arab authorities. Llull also read widely in Christian mystical and apologetic theology, probably relying on texts available from the libraries of local religious houses. His studies seem to have been largely self-guided, and apparently excluded many areas of the liberal arts and higher philosophy that he considered irrelevant to his evangelical project. During this period of preparation, Llull received the inspiration for his famed "Great Universal Art of Finding Truth" (explained below), which he attributed to divine revelation. Around 1275 prince James (soon to become king of Majorca) summoned Llull to Montpellier to have his first writings examined by church authorities. With this departure from his native island, Ramon Llull began a life of virtually constant peregrination.

During the next forty years, Llull traveled constantly, presenting his plans at the courts of Aragon, France, and the papacy; attending meetings of the mendicant orders and other church councils; and making private missionary trips to North Africa and the Eastern Mediterranean. He obtained some support from the Aragonese court: king James II of Majorca founded a center at Miramar to train missionary friars, but this project soon failed; king James II of Aragon granted Llull a small stipend and limited permission to proselytize unbelievers in the royal domain. Llull's greatest success seems to have come at the Council of Vienne of 1311, which decreed the establishment of chairs in Oriental languages at several major universities. Nonetheless, no extant evidence documents Llull's direct participation in the Council or in any other princely or papal undertaking. Indeed, he often complains in his writings that his contemporaries ignore his proposals, and depicts himself as a lone "fool". An intriguing indicator of how Llull's contemporaries saw him appears in a letter of recommendation that he received in 1311 from Francesco Caroccioli, Chancellor of the University of Paris. The Chancellor acknowledges Llull's zeal, but describes his work with a reference to the Gospel parable of the poor widow's mite (Mark 12.42 or Luke 21.2), thus implying that Llull's contributions are meager in substance but rich in spirit. Frustrated by the lack of official response to his proposals, Llull undertook private missions abroad. In late 1315 he made a journey to Tunis, and died in early 1316 either in the North African city or while returning to Majorca , where he lies buried in the church of Saint Francis.

Llull's Oeuvre and the Great Art

Although few of Ramon Llull's contemporaries seem to have paid much attention to him, interest in his work grew continuously in the following century, thanks chiefly to his prodigious written oeuvre. Despite traveling constantly, Llull found time to write nearly 300 works in his native Catalan, in Latin, and in Arabic. No copies of the Arabic versions are known to survive, a loss that has greatly frustrated modern efforts to understand his knowledge of Islamic culture. However, Llull's will provided generously for copying and disseminating his writings, which soon began to circulate throughout Spain, France, and Italy.

Nearly all of Ramon Llull's works offer versions or adaptations of his idiosyncratic theological and philosophical system, the Great Universal Art of Finding Truth. The Great Art synthesizes the methods of contemplation and of evangelical argument that Llull apparently cultivated during his decade of private study. Viewed in its historical context, the Lullian Great Art appears as a comprehensive scheme for achieving the ancient Christian ideal that Saint Bonaventure called "retracing the arts to theology". Llull's system thus constituted a somewhat conservative attempt to maintain the subordination of philosophy to theology and the primacy of cloister over classroom in Western Christian culture. He often recommends his own system as a facile alternative to the academic methods of his day, which he criticizes for abandoning devotion to divine truth in favor of quibbling over human errors (see Oliver and Rodríguez Moreno on Llull's partisan sympathies and polemics).

Ramon Llull's Great Art is a method for discovering how every particular truth, from any field of experience or learning, ultimately manifests the one truth that is God. It accomplishes this by tracing an elaborate web of universal symbolism (explained best by Pring-Mill), whose threads are a fixed set of "Divine Dignities" (attributes of the Godhead). The Dignities constitute the "Absolute Principles" of all being and knowledge. A further set of "Relative Principles" explains the diffusion and operation of the Absolute Principles in various "Subjects" (levels of creation). Finally, a set of "Rules" (heuristic questions) guides inquiry regarding the Principles and Subjects. In the later versions of Llull's Great Art, he identifies nine Principles, Subjects, and Rules, which he symbolizes with the letters B through K of the alphabet, as follows:

ABSOLUTE PRINCIPLES

B	Bonitas [Goodness]
C	Magnitudo [Greatness]
D	Duratio [Eternity]
E	Potestas [Power]
F	Sapientia [Wisdom]
G	Voluntas [Will/Love]
H	Virtus [Virtue]
I	Veritas [Truth]
K	Gloria [Glory]

RELATIVE PRINCIPLES

Differentia [Difference]
Concordantia [Concord]
Contrarietas [Contrariety]
Principium [Beginning]
Medium [Middle]
Finis [End]
Maioritas [Superiority]
Aequalitas [Equality]
Minoritas [Inferiority]

SUBJECTS

B	Deus [God]
C	Angelus [Angel]
D	Homo [Human]
E	Coelum [Heavens]
F	Sensitiva [Senses]
G	Imaginatio [Imagination]
H	Elementativa [Elements]
I	Vegetativa [Vegetal Power]
K	Instrumentativa [Skills & Arts]

RULES

Utrum [Whether?]
Quid [What?]
Quare [Why?]
De Quo [From What?]
Quale [What Kind?]
Quantum [How Much?]
Ubi [Where?]
Quando [When?]
Quomodo et [How and
Cum quo (With What?]

Basic Categories of the Lullian Great Art

Llull's "Figure A"
(The lines connect groups of three Principles)

The letter A is reserved to symbolize the coincidence of all the Principles in God. In the early versions of his Great Art, Llull often uses a more extensive set of alphabetic symbols covering a wide range of theological and philosophical terms. After deciding to limit his alphabet to nine letters, he routinely provides lists of nine Virtues and Vices or of any other nine related categories necessary for specialized application of the Great Art.

Llull's "Combinatory Figure" (the inner circles revolve)

Llull's handling of these symbolic terms does not use the propositional or syllogistic methods of Aristotelian logic. Instead, he combines two or three letters in various "Figures" (circular or tabular diagrams). In later centuries, these Figures inspired great enthusiasm for Llull's system as a virtual "knowledge machine". According to Llull, the resulting letter combinations, such as BD or CFK, constitute true formulations of all possible philosophical and theological propositions. In order to find the truth in these combinations, Llull resorts to a wide range of analogical, allegorical, proportional, and figural arguments (detailed analysis appears in my book on this Lullian "logic"). He insists that these methods constitute "necessary reasons" capable of "demonstrating" the truth of Christian belief to any unbeliever (a claim variously evaluated by Eijo Garay, Gracia, and Mendía). Successful use of the combinatory mechanics and necessary reasons of Llull's Great Art depends almost completely on correct understanding of the meanings that he assigns to the letters B through K. This understanding in turn invariably requires extensive interpretative work, guided by unswerving fidelity to fundamental tenets of Catholic dogma.

Our very limited knowledge about Llull's early years of study and about his subsequent contact with Latin or Arab learning makes it difficult to identify the authors or works that might have inspired the methods of his Great Art. Llull himself almost never cites authorities, perhaps because he attributed his system entirely to divine inspiration, wished to avoid identifying it with other schools of Christian or Islamic thought, or strove to rely solely on necessary reasons. In any case, he routinely recasts all theological and philosophical arguments in the terms of his own Great Art. Later Humanist critics of Llull's system denounced the barbarous absurdity of his contrived terminology and non-Aristotelian argumentation. However, if we recast Llull's ideas in the more conventional language of his contemporaries, his views usually appear quite simplistic and even a little behind the times. Modern scholars sometimes compare his contemplative schemes to those of twelfth-century authors such as Richard of St. Victor. Llull's erudition rarely exceeds the level found in widely-circulated Latin or Arab theological and philosophical compendia. He advances few really original doctrines, although his combinatory methods and necessary reasons do generate several astonishing propositions, such as his theory that speech must be a sixth sense (because it serves to comprehend God just as well as the five bodily senses). Ultimately, if we consider Llull's system in relation to the various philosophical traditions of his era, it appears as a synthesis of orthodox Catholic dogma, basic Neoplatonist metaphysics (as explained in Latin and Arab authorities), and the spiritual psychology of twelfth-century monastic and scholastic writers. The Great Art offers a comprehensive "natural theology", and is perhaps the Christian Middle Age's most ambitious attempt at systematizing the understanding of all creation as "similar and dissimilar symbols" of the Creator (Yates perspicuously studies this heritage).

The practical value of Llull's system is perhaps somewhat easier to appreciate. It probably attracted non-academic lay or clerical readers as a popularized encyclopedia of learning for spiritual edification. In this respect his work most resembles the sermons of mendicant preachers, who created moral allegories from a vast range of learning and lore (see the studies by Bataillon, Delcorno, Rouse, and Zink). This same "moralization" pervades the work of Ramon Llull and similar allegorical methods appear in many other contemporary works of vernacular didactic literature. For example, *Count Lucanor (El Conde Lucanor)*, a collection of exemplary stories by Llull's Castilian contemporary Juan Manuel, includes several sections of obscure ethical proverbs designed to promote moralizing analysis. The *Book of the Lover and the Beloved* serves a similar function. Llull's Great Art exhaustively formalizes these popular applications of moralization into a system that promised to show how every creature from every level of creation offered an opportunity "for knowing and having good moralities" (Llull's label for this process, well analyzed by Cabré et al.).

Llull's Literary Works and the *Book of the Lover and the Beloved*

Most of Ramon Llull's writings offer versions of his Great Art or applications of its methods to particular topics and branches of learning. Some of these consist almost entirely of lists of letter combinations, with little interpretative commentary. However, Llull also wrote a small body of works that modern readers appreciate for their literary qualities. He applied his youthful skill in poetry to composing various religious lyrics and didactic verse primers (although the caliber of his poetic works is not especially high). He also wrote several narrative works, the most celebrated of which are the *Book of Blanquerna (Libre de Blaquerna)* and *Book of Marvels (Libre de meravelles)*. Twentieth-century scholars have dubbed these two texts "spiritual romances" because each one recounts a quest for spiritual perfection by a Christian hero. Both texts construct their plots by concatenating *exempla* of the vices and virtues that their heroes encounter in Christian society, and include other diverse material as well. For example, one section of the *Book of Marvels* is a long fable about the lion as king of beasts. The *Book of Blanquerna* concludes with two sections that offer guides for contemplation, the *Book of the Lover and the Beloved (Libre de amic e amat)* and the *Art of Contemplation (Art de contemplació,* a simplified version of Llull's Great Art). The text presents these guides as compositions created by its protagonist Blanquerna, a "meta-fictional" device for incorporating material that Llull had undoubtedly written independently. Exactly when Ramon Llull completed the *Book of Blanquerna* in its final form remains unclear, although recent scholarship favors a date around 1283 (see Soler). He presumably had already completed the *Book of the Lover and the Beloved.* The *Book of Blanquerna* became one of Llull's most popular works: at least ten medieval manuscript copies survive, including versions in Catalan, French, Provençal, and Latin. The *Book of the Lover and the Beloved* achieved even greater diffusion on its own: Castilian, Catalan, French, and Latin versions circulated in at least sixteen manuscripts (Bonner's *Selected Works* enumerates these). The question of whether Llull composed first the Catalan or Latin version of this text remains undecided, especially since he may have revised either after 1283.

The *Book of Blanquerna* tells how its protagonist, the only child of a wealthy merchant family, abandons worldly affairs with the intention of becoming a hermit. However, his superlative piety and wisdom inevitably lead him to become a monk, abbot, bishop, and eventually pope, offices that he fills with exemplary success. Finally, Blanquerna resigns the Holy See in order to realize his original eremitic aspiration. One of the many "hermits and recluses" living in the "walls of Rome" entreats the former pontiff to become their spiritual leader (Chap. 97.2-3). Blanquerna declines, and retires to an isolated hermitage outside Rome, selected for him by the cardinals and staffed with a single deacon as his attendant. The hermit from Rome later visits Blanquerna seeking a written guide to contemplation, which becomes the *Book of the Lover and the Beloved* (as explained in chapters 99-100, included in the text below). The coincidence between Blanquerna's story and the case of Peter of Morrone, the Italian hermit who served only one year (1294-1295) as Pope Celestine V before resigning, continues to intrigue scholars looking for political or social commentary in Llull's text. Llull clearly esteemed the eremitic vocation, and often makes hermits the mouthpieces of wisdom in his writings (a device studied by Genovart Servera). Indeed, although Pope Alexander IV sought in 1256 to encourage more official organization among hermits by merging several small Italian groups into the single Order of Augustinian Hermits, eremitic retreat remained a common and diversely practiced religious vocation in the Christian West throughout the Middle Ages. The conditions of this vocation might involve complete isolation in a wilderness hermitage, inclosure as an anchorite (often in cells built within the walls of a church or town), living quietly near a religious house, or seclusion in one's own home (a practice called *conversio*, popular among widows and retired couples), all done with varying degrees of official recognition or adherence to a formal religious "rule" (Osheim and Warren study some of these practices). Llull himself apparently lived in a hermitage near a Majorcan religious house during his decade of private study and contemplation (Morey Mora and Seguí analyze this situation). Llull also depicts Blanquerna's parents living as *conversi* after their son leaves home in chapters 4 through 18. Blanquerna's composition of the *Book of the Lover and the Beloved* as a guide for promoting more fervor among religious contemplatives probably reflects contemporary concerns about the rigor of the "rules" followed by so many diverse types of hermits, anchorites, *conversi*, and recluses.

The *Book of the Lover and the Beloved* consists of 366 paragraphs for daily meditation, which it calls "moral metaphors". The narrative introduces this book as a work composed by its protagonist Blanquerna in response to a request from the hermits of Rome, who desired a text to fortify their contemplation and devotion. After pondering the best way to satisfy their request, Blanquerna decided "to make a book about the Lover and the Beloved, in which the Lover is the devout and faithful Christian, and the Beloved is God." Moreover, Blanquerna decided to write this work in the style of the Muslim sufis who offer words of love and brief *exempla* that inspire great devotion and require exposition, in order to spur the mind's ascent to higher thoughts and greater devotion. The *Book of Blanquerna* does not adhere strictly to this meta-fictional conceit. References to the Lover and the Beloved as personifications first appear in Chapter 80, which also tells how pope Blanquerna receives reports about the dreaded assassins and other marvels from Muslim lands. This narrative coincidence perhaps reflects how Llull's own knowledge of the sufis or their practices came from anecdotal reports. Indeed, a later passage (Chap. 88.4) depicts a papal informant obtaining the *Book of the Lover and the Beloved* from Muslims in North Africa. According to the informant, the book tells how "devout men made songs about God and love, and renounced the world for love of God." It speaks approvingly of Muslim preachers who inspire devotion among their audiences, but calls them "tricksters and rogues" (*galiadors e arlots*) without making any reference to the sufis. Llull's claim of a sufist model for the method of his text has attracted considerable attention from modern scholars eager for clues regarding the scope and depth of his knowledge concerning Islam. However, this Muslim spiritual tradition contributes much less to the work's style and content than does traditional Christian spirituality, Ramon Llull's own Great Art, or the courtly love lyric. Before considering the sufist elements in the *Book of the Lover and the Beloved*, it is useful to review the broad contribution of these other discourses.

The contemplative exercises described in the *Book of the Lover and the Beloved*, like the entire system of Llull's Great Art, rely on many commonplace images, models, and methods from Christian devotional literature, spiritual psychology, and exegesis.

The most obvious of these traditional images is Llull's treatment of the human soul as the Lover of God the Beloved. The epithalamic allegory of the relationship between God and the soul was an ancient one, based on exegesis of the Song of Songs already found in Origen and developed especially by Cistercian and Victorine authors of the twelfth century. (Matter surveys these developments). According to Llull's narrative, Blanquerna composed the *Book of the Lover and the Beloved* at the request of hermits, but conceived the figures of the Lover and the Beloved as personifications of any Christian and God. Other Christian Lovers appear in some paragraphs of the text, as do the worldly "people" (often called simply "they") who interrogate, scorn, or abuse the Lover.

Sometimes the Lover is called the "Fool", a label that coincides with Llull's apparent self-representation as "Ramon the Fool" elsewhere in the *Book of Blanquerna* (Chaps. 79.3, 82.6) and reprises the traditional figure of the "divine minstrel" used by Saint Bernard and Saint Francis (see the studies by Leclercq and Corominas). Sometimes the Beloved also appears as the "Lord". Despite these shifts in character, the relationship of the Lover and the Beloved provides the chief continuity in Llull's text. The 366 paragraphs do not form any sequential narrative or dialogue, although occasionally two or more adjoining paragraphs treat the same idea or set of related ideas. Finally, Llull perhaps favored the imagery of the Song of Songs because several of its elements (like the garden and fountain of 4.12 and 4.15) coincide with features from the *locus amoenus* of amorous lyric, which he evokes in many paragraphs.

Equally prominent in Llull's text is his attention to the operation of the Lover's soul. Llull's accounts of spiritual psychology consistently divide the human soul into three main levels — the Senses, Imagination, and Mind. The isolation of Imagination as a separate level is an unconventional doctrine, but clearly helps organize more neatly the mental processes of contemplative ascent and descent that the *Book of the Lover and the Beloved* recommends in order to foster love between humans and their creator (e.g. paragraphs 56 or 258). Llull always divides the Mind into the three faculties of Intellect, Will, and Memory defined by Augustine and repeated by virtually every Christian authority before the thirteenth century. Llull admits only limited elements from the Aristotelian psychology studied so intensely by his Scholastic contemporaries. More often he treats the levels and divisions of the soul as virtual personifications, like protagonists in a spiritual psychomachia.

He insists that all three faculties of the mind contribute equally to the soul's grasp of
God, (paragraphs 19, 123, 198, 241, and 288). Yet Llull argues as well that the
Intellect must guide the Will, Memory, Imagination, and Senses, so that
understanding can lead faith. (The latter claim encouraged later medieval critics of his
work to denounce him as a heretical "rationalist".) Llull's treatment of spiritual
psychology often seems almost mechanistic, with little attention to the paradoxes of
ineffability or flights of ecstasy that we consider characteristic of mysticism. Indeed,
Llull very rarely uses the word "mystic" in his writings, and never advocates any true
experience of fusion with the Divine Being. Instead Llull's text stresses several
broader devotional ideals. The most prominent is of course the love of God (analyzed
by Oltra, Sala-Molins, and Serverat). Many paragraphs express the conviction that
Christians should love God simply in response to divine goodness, rather than from
fear of eternal punishment (e.g. paragraphs 218 and 239). Since this love is a
function of the Will in Llull's spiritual psychology, he repeatedly emphasizes the
operation of that faculty, and especially the exercise of free will (e.g. paragraphs 307,
310, 311, 318-19, or 321). Several paragraphs describe the surrender of the will to
God with the image of the slave (e.g 220, 243, 295, or 319), echoing Saint Paul's
famous "slave of Christ" (1 Corinthians 7.22). The Lover's devotion should be so
intense that he will accept martyrdom or abuse for the sake of the Beloved (as
suggested in paragraph 11). Only slightly less important than the duty and practice
of love is the anguish of penitential compunction. This arises from two causes:
first, the Lover's distress over separation from the Beloved, especially when caused by
the Lover's failings; second, the Lover's grief over the dishonor done to the Beloved
when Christians allow unbelievers to ignore His love (as argued in paragraphs 99 and
218). Llull's concern for this dishonor adumbrates the penitential theme that
misconduct by contemporary sinners prolongs Christ's Passion, which became
especially widespread in later medieval devotion (as Kieckheffer explains).
Expression of penitence through weeping was an ideal of monastic devotion since the
era of Saint Gregory (a tradition well summarized by Leclercq's *Love of Learning*) and
Llull's text frequently illustrates this "lachrymal piety". Finally, the *Book of the
Lover and the Beloved* sometimes offers straightforward instruction in basic Christian
doctrines such as free will or the Last Judgement (paragraphs 318 and 353), a
catechetical function found in many of Llull's other devotional writings.
    The devotional value of the *Book of the Lover and the Beloved* is also profoundly
indebted to traditional Christian exegetical methods. Llull often recommends using
difficult language to stimulate the mind's grasp of higher truths (a function analyzed
in detail in my study of his rhetoric). The allegorical value of obscure language was
virtually an axiom of ancient literary culture, inherited by both Christians and
Muslims. Its elaboration by patristic authorities such as Augustine and Gregory
made it a foundation of Scriptural exegesis in monastic culture and eventually of
Scholastic exegesis and popular preaching alike in Llull's era (an evolution well
traced by Smalley). Compilations of exegetical interpretations (*distinctiones*)
circulated widely as sourcebooks of allegorical lore: references to this exegesis in
notes on Llull's text refer to meanings found in the *Allegoriae* of Pseudo-Rabanus
and the *Distinctiones* of Alan of Lille, printed in Patrologia Latina, volumes 112:
849-1088 and 210: 686-1612. The *Book of the Lover and the Beloved* in effect offers

devout laypeople the opportunity to practice a less rigorous form of monastic meditative reading (a function of much vernacular devotional literature and art, well explained by Bartlett and Gillespie). Several of the text's "moral metaphors" mention this use of spiritual vision in order to transcend material images (e.g. paragraphs 40, 144, 265-66, 270, or 285). The *Book of the Lover and the Beloved* attempts to merge this practice of higher insight with the soul's desire for God, in order to create a comprehensive mystical art.

Terms and themes from Llull's Great Art recur throughout the *Book of the Lover and the Beloved*. Many passages invoke the mechanics of his system: for example, paragraph 205 on affirmation and negation or paragraphs 289-90 on possibility, impossibility, difference, and agreement. The love between Lover and Beloved, like all relations between creature and Creator, necessarily occurs through the influence of the Lullian Principles (see paragraph 83). Llull's chief discursive device for expressing this influence is repetitive use of his system's terminology. Thus paragraph 305 repeatedly refers to his Principle of Greatness and paragraph 297 invokes many types of Eternity. At least one modern scholar (Hatzfeld), unaware of the methods of Llull's Great Art, regarded this repetition as the expression of Llull's own mystical ecstasies. Most passages in the *Book of the Lover and the Beloved* explicitly treat Llull's favorite spiritual concerns, like converting unbelievers, reforming Christian society, and guiding the soul to know, love, and praise God. The text's treatment of these common, orthodox goals, largely unhindered by Llull's idiosyncratic terminology, perhaps helps to explain the modest success of the *Book of the Lover and the Beloved* among later medieval readers.

Llull's youthful interest in the courtly love lyric presumably familiarized him with its conventional themes and vocabulary. Echoes of these appear scattered throughout the *Book of the Lover and the Beloved*. Various passages employ nature imagery favored by the troubadours: birds singing, dawn, and the *loci amoeni* of gardens or fountains. Other commonplace themes from courtly love literature include the lover's illness, the prison of love, the fire of love, the Lover as servant of the Beloved, the lover's suffering, the paradoxes of love, and the secret character of love. Llull's use of imagery associated with courtly love especially suggests that his intended readership was not simply religious but devout laypeople familiar with such material (devotional literature of the era often employs such imagery, as Bartlett explains). In addition, a very high proportion of the "moral metaphors" in Llull's text consist of paradoxes, particularly dilemmas that contrast two equally tenable or untenable situations. This preference parallels the taste for verbal puzzles, riddles, and obscure images often found in troubadour lyrics as well as much popular didactic literature. The sententious quality of many passages in the *Book of the Lover and the Beloved* also recalls the numerous guides to courtesy composed of proverbs, a genre that Llull cultivated by creating several collections of sayings and maxims.

Finally, the sufist features of the *Book of the Lover and the Beloved* remain the most intriguing yet difficult to assess, partly due to our limited knowledge of Llull's familiarity with Islamic literature and partly due to the wide range of practices embraced by sufism, which is scarcely less capacious than the category "mysticism" itself (as Baldick argues). Moreover, the distinctive practices, themes, or ideals of the various sufist schools or "brotherhoods" often have Christian parallels. Indeed, given the sufis' widespread and prominent role in Islamic culture, it is surprising that their mention in the *Book of the Lover and the Beloved* is the only obvious reference to them from Llull's entire oeuvre. It is possible that he knew them only because of the coincidence between his esteem for obscure language and their reputed use of provocative *exempla*. Some sufist groups did especially encourage the cultivation of poetry as a vehicle for attaining higher knowledge: for example, Llull's Indian contemporary Nasir al-Din of Delhi (died 1356) developed a sophisticated doctrine for "relating" descriptions of human beauty or lines of verse to God's attributes. It is difficult to know whether Llull's phrase "moral metaphors" specifically refers to any doctrines of this kind: lacking advanced training in grammar or exegesis, he typically uses the terms "moral" and "metaphor" very broadly to indicate any edifying truth and any figurative discourse.

The sufist inspiration for Llull's text is even more difficult to assess with respect to his treatment of the Lover and the Beloved as masculine figures. Although Llull gives these personifications overtly Christian meanings (the Beloved is God and the Lover is the Christian), his usage also coincides with that of the Classical Arabic love lyrics directed by men to boys. Presentation of the Lover and Beloved as masculine typically appears in sufist works that use love for handsome boys (and human beauty in general) to exemplify how all created beauty engages divine beauty. This tactic appears even in the work of sufi authorities who specifically denounce love for boys in practice (Baldick cites the case of the eleventh-century Iranian author Qushayri). Llull's *Book of the Lover and the Beloved* also frequently refers to God's beauty, but typically as an "excellence" of divine existence alone, without reference to corresponding human or mundane manifestations of beauty. Moreover, Llull's text stresses the triadic relationship of Love, Lover, and Beloved, which is an ancient and widely developed theme in both Christian and Islamic spiritual literature. Finally, the representation of intense affection between male figures commonly (if not necessarily) occurs in many other Christian devotional genres, from the letters of spiritual friendship among monks to the songs of praise (*laude*) addressed to God by the all-male Italian confraternities. Llull himself uses the terms "lover" (*amic*) and "beloved" (*amat*) to discuss the Christian ideal of love for one's neighbor in chapter 307 of his early *Book of Contemplation on God* (*Libre de contemplació en Déu*, in volume 7 of the Catalan *Obres*). In short, it is difficult to know whether Llull was even aware of the connection between his terminology and the theme of love for boys in Arab culture.

There are various other thematic coincidences between Llull's *Book of the Lover and the Beloved* and basic sufist doctrines, most of which demonstrate common features of Christian and Muslim ascetic spirituality. Many passages in Llull's text refer to the Lover traveling a road: sufist authors traditionally call their way of life (or any of its specific schools) the "Path". Llull's attention to stages in the Lover's quest for the Beloved and to affective processes in the Lover's soul parallel the traditional sufist concern for the so-called penitential "stations" (such as repentance, poverty, patience, or trust in God) and mystic "states" (such as watchfulness, nearness, love, fear, hope, intimacy, tranquility, or contemplation). These lead ultimately to some experience of "certainty", "passing away" or "survival" in God, which perhaps matches the loss of self or "death" described at several points in Llull's text (for example, paragraphs 54 and 171). Like Llull, most sufi authors do not regard this ultimate state as a unitive fusion with the divine. The Lover's willingness to appear a "fool" and to incur ridicule from others also recalls those sufist masters that advocate drawing blame on oneself as a means of renouncing the world. The *Book of the Lover and the Beloved* often refers to the "secrets" of love between the Lover and the Beloved; likewise, various sufist authors discuss the "secrets" between God and "God's friends" (as the sufis often call themselves). Finally, the reference to inebriation in paragraph 364 from Llull's text offers an especially intriguing coincidence with another basic sufist theme. Two major divisions in sufism are the so-called "sober" and "drunken" schools: the former favors goals of quietism and Stoic-like renunciation (to use Western terms), while the latter encourages ecstatic and trance-like experiences (most famously the dances of the "whirling dervishes"). Many sufist writers of the latter tendency thus expound themes of drinking and drunkenness. All these topics are commonplaces that individual sufist authorities develop in much more detailed doctrines. At the same time, there are many striking and widespread sufist practices that have no parallels in Llull's text, such as their organization into brotherhoods and lodges, the ecstatic behaviour of the dervishes, or the repetition of formulaic phrases for "remembering" God, to name just a few.

Since sufism was such a varied and widespread practice within Islam, it is hard to claim that Llull's reference to one sufist practice alone (the use of obscure language) demonstrates any profound debt to specific sufist writings. At the same time, he may well have known of sufist practices from contemporary Hispanoarab culture: the great Spanish-born sufist authority Ibn Arabi (died 1240) describes some remarkable sufi devotional practices among the artisan and working classes of Muslim Spain. At the very least, Llull's own experiences abroad or the reports of missionaries and merchants could have furnished him with anecdotal information about sufism (although popular medieval Christian conceptions of Muslim practices were often as mistaken as Muslim views of Christian behavior, as Urvoy has shown). Still, the fact remains that Llull offers few recognizable allusions to sufi-like practices elsewhere in his oeuvre. Instead, his writings almost always focus on those Islamic theological and philosophical tenets that most directly oppose Christian doctrines regarding the Trinity and the Incarnation (analyzed by Burman). Ultimately, then, it is difficult to accept modern claims about the pervasive Islamic inspiration of Llull's text; such claims involve assumptions about the impact of cultural "otherness" that belong more to twentieth-century "orientalism" than to the ideals of thirteenth-century evangelism. Llull certainly did not write the *Book of the Lover and the Beloved* as a kind of "Trojan Horse" for introducing sufist doctrines into Christian belief. Instead, his interest in their doctrines may have arisen because he knew that orthodox Muslims criticized more heterodox sufis for accepting some Christian beliefs, and thus he regarded the sufis as an especially favorable audience for proselytizing. In the end, Llull's citation of the sufis may simply illustrate contemporary Christian moralists' predilection for invoking examples of "virtuous pagans" to castigate sinful Christian audiences (a theme well studied by Vitto). He includes just such a moralizing 'reference to Muslim practice in paragraph 154. Viewed most generously, Llull's approval of the sufis or other Muslim practices expresses his general conviction that a common desire for the Supreme Good must exist among all humans. At the very least, his reference to the sufis is an interesting indicator of the "popular ethnography" concerning Islam that circulated among educated European laypeople of his era.

About this Translation

Many English-speaking students of medieval spiritual literature first encountered Ramon Llull's *Book of the Lover and the Beloved* in the translation published by E. Allison Peers in 1923. Peers's version contributed substantially to interest in all of Llull's work, and remained in print (with some revisions) for almost five decades. When the last reprinting of Peers's text ceased to be available, the need for a new version soon became obvious. At least one new English translation for general readers has already appeared. My new translation aims to serve both a general audience as well as readers with a more specialized interest in Llull's work or Eve Bonner's in medieval history and literature.

Ramon Llull was one of the first and most prolific medieval European authors to use a vernacular language for treating theological and philosophical issues, which were usually expounded in Latin. His frequent recourse to neologisms in Catalan indicates the challenge of this undertaking. There was, broadly speaking, no established "high style" available in Catalan for Llull to employ; he probably preferred to maintain a simpler, more popularizing diction in any case. The Latin version of the *Book of the Lover and the Beloved* also employs a very plain style, largely devoid of the poetical or rhetorical embellishments taught in the schools. Llull's vernacular text does, however, use the long sentence structure typical of thirteenth-century Catalan prose idiom. E. Allison Peers's translation rendered this idiom in an admirably literal fashion: however, by reproducing very closely in English the syntax of the original Catalan, it created an extremely formal tone. This new English translation consequently employs either paratactic paraphrases or elliptical constructions more appropriate to modern popular English. At the same time, it avoids using English idiomatic phrases that might introduce false connotations into Llull's typically spare and allusive language. The English combines details from both the Catalan and Latin texts, since these often differ somewhat. (Medieval translations between the vernacular and Latin often seem more like paraphrase, rather than word-for-word renderings.) In general, this version strives to reproduce the uncomplicated tenor of Llull's original text through simple (though not colloquial) diction, while also respecting its conceptual integrity and lofty sense of "moral metaphor". This is particularly critical to reproducing the fundamental idea, concept, image or word-play that typically constitutes the key to understanding each paragraph, which is supposed to require exposition in the manner of the expressions of sufi holy men. Therefore this translation strictly avoids expanding those metaphorical, allusive, or symbolic elements that *ought* to exercise the reader's interpretative imagination; notes to the text help to elucidate Llull's allegory or arguments. In the best of all possible linguistic universes, the ideal way of rendering Llull's little paragraphs might be to recast them as riddles, proverbs, or jokes that employ a colloquial idiom to imply a profound moral truth.

The *Book of the Lover and the Beloved* includes relatively little of the notoriously idiosyncratic and complicated terminology used in Llull's theological and philosophical treatises. This translation attempts to replicate the distinctive spiritual vocabulary that Llull does employ, so that readers can appreciate as fully as possible the details of his mystical psychology and theology. For this reason many of the Catalan or Latin terms that Llull commonly uses appear rendered more or less literally with their English cognates. Unfortunately, some of these words have very different connotations in modern English usage. This includes one of Llull's favorite terms, the noun and verb "languish" (Catalan *languor* or *languiment* and *languir*; Latin *langor* and *languire*). Because these words are so prominent in Llull's spiritual vocabulary, this translation retains them as the noun "anguish" and verb "languish". Similarly, the Catalan term *pensaments* or Latin term *cogitationes* (literally "thoughts") almost always appears in English as "cares", because this word best expresses the sense of preoccupation in the Lover's penitential meditations. Other words, such as the nouns "tribulation" or "travail", are now very rare or specialized in English. None the less, students of medieval religious literature should readily recognize these terms in the sense that Llull uses them. It seems desirable to maintain them, as obsolete or specialized as they are, for their historical value as indicators of Llull's spiritual values and ideals. This translation attempts to incorporate them as smoothly as possible into its otherwise modern idiom, with the hope that their repeated use will naturalize them in this context for current readers.

Equally challenging to modern readers may be the Scholastic theological or philosophical vocabulary that Llull often employs. Wherever possible, this translation attempts to use such terms consistently, so that a modern reader can recognize their special value in Llull's arguments. In order to reproduce as exactly as possible Llull's spiritual psychology, this English rendering capitalizes and preserves without substitution the names of the three Augustinian faculties of the soul: Intellect, Will, and Memory. In general, whenever Llull's text mentions "understanding", "wanting" or "desiring", and "remembering", it indicates the specific operation of the Intellect, Will, and Memory, respectively. Some sections of the text include specialized terminology from Scholastic logic and metaphysics. These also appear rendered in modern English cognates that correspond more or less to the original medieval concept; occasionally a note helps explain the doctrine that Llull's text invokes.

As inevitably occurs in any translation, some words simply cannot pass readily from one language into another. In Llull's text, the Catalan terms *honors, honraments, dignitats* and *nobilitat* and their Latin cognates present such a problem: they indicate literally the great honor, dignity, or exalted status of someone occupying a high social or political rank. Adapting the English honorific "excellency", this translation usually renders these terms with the word "excellence". Similar use of the Catalan term *valors* (literally "values" or "worths") poses less difficulty, because it corresponds readily to the English "worthiness". In any case, it is important to notice that Llull uses terms such as "valor", "honor", "nobility", "virtue", "excellence", "complement" and "perfection" almost interchangeably as names for the attributes of the Godhead. These words thus serve in the *Book of the Lover and the Beloved* as surrogates for his Divine Dignities or Absolute Principles. The Dignities themselves often appear as adjectives, adverbs, or even proper names attributed to either creatures or their Creator.

Finally, because Llull's text presents both the Lover and the Beloved as masculine, confusion might arise from the frequent unclarified use of the pronouns "he" or "him" and the adjective "his". Consequently, these words appear capitalized wherever they indicate the Beloved. To provide further variation and to avoid gender-specific diction, this translation uses neutral terms like "people" to render collective terms like the Catalan *homens* or Latin *homines* ("men"). Llull's text itself frequently uses the indefinite "they".

About this Edition

Several modern critical editions of the Catalan version of the *Book of the Lover and the Beloved* have appeared. One modern edition of the Latin text is also available. The aim of this trilingual edition is not to supplant these critical redactions of the text, but simply to provide accurate copies of the Catalan and Latin versions for readers with competence in these languages. This edition transcribes the Catalan and Latin versions found in two of the oldest extant manuscripts. The Catalan text comes from Munich, Bayerische Staatsbibliothek, Cod. hisp. 67, ff. 201r-232r. This early fourteenth-century manuscript is a modestly prepared copy of the *Book of Blanquerna*, written in a large, very clear bookhand with regular rubrication. There are few corrections or marginalia. The Latin version comes from a very different type of manuscript: Venice, Biblioteca Nazionale Marciana, MS lat. VI.200 (2757), ff. 188rb-195rb. This is a professionally copied deluxe collection of Llull's works, which he commisioned for presentation to the Doge of Venice in 1298 (the front flyleaf bears what some scholars consider Llull's autograph dedication). Almost all the texts in this volume appear copied in two columns per page, using a small, highly abbreviated bookhand, extensive red and blue rubrication, and different sizes of initial capitals, often with elaborate flourishes of tracery. Some works in the collection bear occasional corrections or marginalia in a similar small hand, as well as a few emendations in various later hands.

Twentieth-century critical editions of Llull's Catalan and Latin texts offer modern scholars' idealized reconstructions of his original composition. The versions provided here offer Llull's work in the much less perfect form that medieval readers knew it. This choice does not reflect any special zeal for historical authenticity, but simply an expedient way of providing readers with a basis for their own study and judgement of the text. These transcriptions are perhaps an especially appropriate means of studying a work that invites its readers to puzzle over its sense, and which served as an instrument for intense practical devotion as much as a record for occasional reference or study. The transcriptions in this edition follow the manuscripts very closely in rubrication, punctuation, capitalization, apparent scribal errors, and textual divergences. Brief indications of these lapses appear in brackets, as does the foliation from each manuscript. The Catalan manuscript displays rather anarchic word separation and frequent alternation in its use of "j" for "i" or "v" for "u". The transcription regularizes these features to match their presumed pronunciation, and resolves all abbreviations. However, the orthography of contracted articles, pronouns, possessive adjectives, and prepositions remains as given in the manuscript, since regularizing their diverse combinations would require many

xxvi

changes in the text as written. The Latin manuscript is much more regular in word separation and orthography. The transcription resolves its numerous abbreviations; it also regularizes the alternation between "j" and "i" or "v" and "u" (but not between "c" and "t").

The division of the text into paragraphs for daily meditation appears to be defective in both manuscripts, even though they clearly mark those divisions: the Catalan volume uses paragraph symbols and the Latin volume large initial letters to introduce each new paragraph. As the transcriptions show, these symbols and initials diverge at 23 points. The Latin text in fact lacks two paragraphs (221 and 284) found in the Catalan. Nonetheless, the two versions synoptically define 363 divisions. This edition adds three more (paragraphs 66, 83, and 95), following conjectures originally offered in the edition by Galmés and Ferrà, and based on obvious parallels in phrasing with other paragraphs. This emendation is justified since Llull uses 366 divisions in his other works of this kind, most notably his massive *Book of Contemplation on God* (*Libre de contemplació en Déu*). It seems capricious to adopt the solution of the Latin text's modern editors, who divide the work into 354 sections corresponding to the days in the Muslim calendar. This solution appears especially incongruous, since Llull's narrative presents the *Book of the Lover and the Beloved* as a text for use by Christian hermits in Rome.

Acknowledgements

This edition would never have appeared were it not for the suggestion of Professor Valerie Lagorio, eminent scholar of medieval mystical literature, now retired from the University of Iowa. Discovering in 1990 that Peers's translation of the *Book of the Lover and the Beloved* was no longer in print, she asked me to make a new translation for use in her classes. Studying a subject as diverse and difficult as Ramon Llull necessarily relies on assistance from many other scholars and institutions. Grants from the Newberry Library in Chicago and from Illinois State University afforded me the time and resources needed to expand my original translation into this trilingual edition. The Bayerische Staatsbibliothek in Munich and the Biblioteca Nazionale Marciana in Venice very promptly provided microfilms of the necessary manuscripts. Lucinda Phillips of Aris and Phillips has enthusiastically supported this project from its first stages of preparation to its final production. Finally, I owe particular thanks for the many small encouragements given by John Bollweg, Tom Burman, Paul Gehl, Joe Gwara, Donna Rogers, Larry Simon, Barry Taylor, and my wife, Anne Clark Bartlett. May their several Paths all lead to the Perfection of Perfections!

MDJ, Chicago, October 1995

Bibliography

I. Studies on Ramon Llull and His Work

An enormous body of literature on Ramon Llull has appeared since the sixteenth century. In general, the works produced before this century are useful only as historical testimony to the spread of Lullism itself. Many recent non-scholarly works still repeat legendary or apocryphal material from earlier texts. The following list offers a guide to selected works from reliable modern scholarship.

Bibliographies

Brummer, Rudolf. *Bibliographia Lulliana: Ramon-Llull-Schrifttum 1870-1973.* Hildesheim: H. Gerstenberg, 1976.

Salleras i Carolà, Marcel. "Bibliografia lul.liana (1974-1984)." *Randa* 19 (1986): 153-98.

Studia Lulliana (Formerly titled *Estudios Lulianos,* this journal lists new Lullian scholarship in each issue.)

Editions of Llull's Writings

Nova edició de les obres de Ramon Llull. 2 vols. to date. Palma de Mallorca: Patronat Ramon Llull, 1990- . (This Catalan series continues the *Obres originals.)*

Obres essencials. Ed. Miquel Batllori et al. 2 vols. Barcelona: Selecta, 1957-61. (Catalan)

Obres de Ramon Lull. Ed. M. Obrador y Benassar, Salvador Galmés, et al. 21 vols. Palma de Mallorca: Comissió Editora Lulliana, 1906-17 and Diputació Provincial de Balears and Institut d'Estudis Catalans, 1923-50. (Catalan)

Opera Latina. 18 vols. to date. Palma de Mallorca: Maioricensis Schola Lullistica del CSIC, 1959-67; Turnhout: Brepols, 1978- . (All volumes since the sixth of this Latin edition have appeared in the Corpus Christianorum, Continuatio Mediaevalis.)

Opera omnia. Ed. Ivo Salzinger. 9 vols. Mainz, 1721-40; rprt. Frankfurt am Main: Minerva, 1965. (This Latin edition includes many works still not printed elsewhere.)

Selected Works of Ramon Llull. Tr. Anthony Bonner. Princeton: Princeton UP, 1985. (English)

Editions and Translations of the
Book of the Lover and the Beloved

Bonner, Eve. *The Book of the Lover and the Beloved.* In *Doctor Illuminatus: A Ramon Llull Reader.* Ed. Anthony Bonner. Princeton: Princeton UP, 1993. Pp. 173-237. (English)

Galmés, Salvador and Miquel Ferrà. *Libre de Blanquerna.* Obres de Ramon Lull 9. Palma de Mallorca: Comissió Editora Lulliana, 1914. Pp. 379-431. (Catalan)

Grifeu, Patrick. *Livre de l'ami et de l'aimé.* Lyon: Orphée/La Différence, 1989. (French)

Lohr, Charles and Fernando Domínguez. "Raimundus Lullus, 'Liber amici et amati': Introduction and Critical Text." *Traditio* 44 (1988): 325-72. (Latin)

Olivar, Marçal. *Llibre d'amic e amat. Llibre d'Ave Maria.* Els Nostres Clàssics14. Barcelona: Els Nostres Clàssics, 1927. 7-105. (Catalan)

Peers, E. Allison. *The Book of the Lover and the Beloved.* New York: Macmillan, 1923. (English)

Riquer, Martín and Lola Badía. *Libro de amigo y Amado.* Barcelona: Planeta, 1985. (Spanish)

Sala-Molins, Louis. *L'arbre de philosophie d'amour, Le livre de l'ami et de l'aimé et choix de textes.* Paris: Aubier-Montaigne, 1967. (French)

Comprehensive Studies of Llull's Career

Batllori, Miquel. *Ramon Llull en el món del seu temps.* Barcelona: Rafael Dalmau, 1961.

---------- and J. N. Hillgarth, ed. *Vida de Ramon Llull: les fonts escrites i la iconografia coetànies.* Barcelona: Associació de Bibliòfils de Barcelona, 1982.

Bonner, Anthony, tr. *Selected Works of Ramon Llull.* Princeton: Princeton UP, 1985. 3-89.

---------- and Lola Badia. *Ramon Llull: Vida, pensament i obra literària.* Barcelona: Empúries, 1988.

Carreras y Artau, Joaquín & Tomás. *Historia de la filosofía española.* 2 vols. Madrid: Asociación Española para el Progreso de las Ciencias, 1939-43. 1: 233-646.

Hillgarth, Joceyln N. *Ramon Lull and Lullism in Fourteenth-Century France.* Oxford: Clarendon Press, 1971.

Platzeck, Erhard-Wolfram. *Raimund Lull. Sein Leben--Seine Werke. Die Grundlagen seines Denkens (Prinzipienlehre).* 2 vols. Rome: Editiones Franciscanae & Düsseldorf: Verlag L. Schwann, 1962-4.

Studies on Major Aspects of Llull's Work

Burman, Thomas E. "The Influence of the *Apology of Al-Kindi* and *Contrarietas Alfolica* on Ramon Lull's Late Religious Polemics, 1305-1313." *Mediaeval Studies* 53 (1991): 197-228.

Cabré, Lluis, et al. "'Conèixer e haver moralitats bones': L'us de la literatura en *L'Arbre exemplifical* de Ramon Llull." *Estudios Lulianos* 28 (1988): 139-67.

Corominas, Juan. "El juglar a lo divino en la vida y en la obra de Ramon Llull." In *Actas del I Congreso Internacional sobre la juglaresca.* Ed. Manuel Criado de Val. Madrid: EDI-6, 1986. Pp. 253-64.

Eijo Garay, Leopoldo. "Las 'razones necesarias' del Beato Ramón Llull en el marco de su época," *Estudios Lulianos* 9 (1965): 23-38.

Garcías Palou, Sebastián. *Ramon Llull y el Islam.* Palma de Mallorca: Institut d'Estudis Balears, 1981.

Genovart Servera, Gabriel. "El Cavaller i el Vell Savi (imatges i símbols de la pedagogia lul.liana)." *Estudis Baleàrics* 2 (1982): 59-75.

Gracia, Jorge. "The Structural Elements of Necessary Reasons in Anselm and Llull." *Diálogos* 9 (1973): 105-29.

Grieve, Hermann. "Ramon Llull i la càbala." *Calls* 3 (1988): 75-82.

Hillgarth, J. N. "La Biblioteca de la Real: fuentes posibles de Llull." *Estudios Lulianos* 7 (1963): 5-17.

Homage to Ramon Llull. Special issue of *Catalan Review* 4 (1990).

Imbach, Ruedi et al. *Raymond Lulle: Christianisme, Judaïsme, Islam. Les Actes du Colloque sur R. Lulle, Université de Fribourg, 1984.* Fribourg: Editions Universitaires, 1986.

Johnston, Mark D. *The Evangelical Rhetoric of Ramon Llull.* New York: Oxford UP, 1995.

----------. "Ramon Llull's Conversion to Penitence." *Mystics Quarterly* 16 (1990): 179-92.

----------. *The Spiritual Logic of Ramon Llull.* Oxford: Clarendon Press, 1987.

Lohr, Charles. "Christianus arabicus cuius nomen Raimundus Lullus." *Freiburger Zeitschrift für Philosophie und Theologie* 31 (1984): 57-88.

Mendía, Benito. "En torno a las razones necesarias de la Apologética Luliana." *Verdad y Vida* 8 (1950): 385-421.

Monserrat Quintana, Antonio. *La visión luliana del mundo del derecho.* Palma de Mallorca: Institut d'Estudis Balearics, 1987.

Moreno Rodríguez, Felipe. *La lucha de Ramon Llull contra el averroísmo entre 1.309 y 1.311.* Madrid: U Complutense de Madrid, 1982.

Morey Mora, Guillem. "La localització del primitiu ermitatge de Ramon Llull al Puig de Randa." *Estudios Lulianos* 28 (1988): 39-49.

Oliver, Antonio. "El Beato Ramón Llull en sus relaciones con la escuela franciscana de los siglos XIII-XIV." *Estudios Lulianos* 9 (1965): 55-70 & 145-65; 10 (1966): 49-56; 11 (1967): 89-119; 13 (1969): 51-65.

Pring-Mill, Robert D. F. "The Analogical Structure of the Lullian Art." In *Islamic Philosophy and the Classical Tradition: Essays Presented to Richard Walzer.* Columbia, SC: U South Carolina P, 1973. Pp. 315-26.

----------. *El microcosmos lul:lià.* Oxford: Dolphin, 1961.
----------. "The Trinitarian World-Picture of Ramón Lull." *Romanistisches Jahrbuch* 7 (1955-56): 229-56.
Raymond Lulle et le Pays d'Oc. Cahiers de Fanjeaux 22. Toulouse: E. Privat, 1987.
Rubió i Balaguer, Jordi. *Ramon Llull i el lul.lisme.* Montserrat: Publicacions de l'Abadia de Montserrat, 1985.
Sala-Molins, Louis. *La philosophie de l'amour chez Raymond Lulle.* Paris: Mouton, 1974.
Seguí, G. "La influencia cisterciense en el Bto. R. Llull," *Estudios Lulianos* 1 (1957): 351-70 and 2 (1958): 245-72.
Sugranyes de Franch, Ramon. *Raymond Lulle Docteur des Missions avec un choix de textes traduits et annotés.* Fribourg: Nouvelle Revue de Science Missionaire, 1954.
Tusquets, Joan. *Ramon Llull pedagogo de la cristiandad.* Madrid: CSIC, 1954.
Urvoy, Dominique. *Penser l'islam: les présupposés islamiques de l'"Art" de Lull.* Paris: J. Vrin, 1980.
----------. "Ramon Llull et l'Islam." *Islamochristiana* 7 (1981): 127-146.
Yates, Frances A. "The Art of Ramon Lull." *Journal of the Warburg and Courtauld Institute* 17 (1954): 115-73.
----------. "Ramón Llull y Johannes Scotus Eriugena." *Estudios Lulianos* 6 (1962): 71-82.

Specialized Studies on the *Book of the Lover and the Beloved*

Dolç, Miquel. "Ocells i arbres en el *Llibre d'Amic e Amat.*" *Estudis Romanics* 10 (1962): 63-71]
Domínguez, Fernando. "El *Libre de amic e Amat.* Reflexions entorn de Ramon Llull i la seva obra literària." *Randa* 19 (1986): 111-35.
Johnston, Mark D. "Ramon Llull's Language of Contemplation and Action." *Forum for Modern Language Studies* 27 (1991): 100-12.
Lorenz, Erika. "Die Analogie der Sehnsucht im *Libre de amic e amat*: Zur Erhellung der Werkstruktur." In Bernhard Konig et al., ed. *Gestaltung-Umgestaltung: Beiträge zur Geschichte der romanischen Literaturen.* Tubingen: Narr; 1990. Pp. 175-83.
Nicolau, Miguel. "La mística de Ramón Llull en el Libro 'Del Amigo y del Amado'." *Estudios Lulianos* 24 (1980): 129-63.
Oltra, Miguel. "La teoría del amor, en el 'Libro del amigo y del amado', de Ramon Llull." *Estudios Lulianos* 17 (1973): 179-91.
Platzeck, E.-W. "La contemplación religiosa de Ramon Llull en los primeros años de su actividad literaria (1271-1276)." *Estudios Lulianos* 22 (1978): 87-115.
Pring-Mill, R. D. F. "Entorn de la unitat del 'Libre d'amich e amat'." *Estudis Romànics* 10 (1962): 33-61.
Sala-Molins, Louis. "Mystique byzantine et mystique lullienne: Raymond Lulle et Gregoire Palamas." *Estudios Lulianos* 7 (1963): 53-74.

----------. "Le refus de l'identification dans la mystique lullienne." *Estudios Lulianos* 9 (1965): 39-53 & 181-92.

Sancho, A. "La mística de Raimundo Lulio." *Revista de espiritualidad* 2 (1943): 19-34.

Serverat, Vincent. "Autour de la notion de l'amitié dans le *Libre d'amic e amat.*" *Estudios Lulianos* 29 (1989): 125-45.

Soler i Llompart, Albert. "Encara sobre la data del *Blaquerna.*" *Studia Lulliana* 31 (1991): 113-23.

----------. "'Enfre la vinya e.l fenollar'? La composició del 'Libre d'amic e amat' i l'experiència mística de Ramon Llull." *Caplletra* 13 (Tardor 1992): 13-22.

Urvoy, Dominique. "Les emprunts mystiques entre Islam et Christianisme et la véritable portée du *Libre d'Amic.*" *Estudios Lulianos* 23 (1979): 37-44.

Valdivieso, L. Teresa. "Exegesis escritural de la producción luliana ." In *II Jornadas de Literatura Española Medieval, Buenos Aires, Argentina 1987.* Ed. L. Teresa Valdivieso & Jorge H. Valdivieso. Buenos Aires: U. Católica Argentina, 1988. Pp. 125-31.

II. Studies on Christian Spirituality, Sufism, and Christian-Muslim Relations in Llull's Era

The literature regarding these fields is vast. The following very selective list indicates only a few studies of particular relevance to Llull's activities and Muslim Spain.

Arié, Rachel. *Etudes sur la civilisation de l'Espagne musulmane.* Leiden: E.J. Brill, 1990.

Baldick, Julian. *Mystical Islam: An Introduction to Sufism.* New York: New York UP, 1989.

Bartlett, Anne Clark. *Male Authors, Female Readers: Representation and Subjectivity in Middle English Literature.* Ithaca, NY: Cornell UP, 1995.

Bataillon, Louis-Jacques. *La prédication au XIIIe siècle en France et Italie.* Brookfield, VT: Ashgate Variorum, 1993.

Burman, Thomas. *Religious Polemic and the Intellectual History of the Mozarabs, c. 1050-1200.* Leiden: E. J. Brill, 1994.

Burns, Robert I. "Christian Islamic Confrontation in the West: The Thirteenth-century Dream of Conversion." *American Historical Review* 76 (1971): 1386-1434.

----------. *Islam under the Crusaders: Colonial Survival in the Thirteenth-Century Kingdom of Valencia.* Princeton: Princeton UP, 1973.

Chejne, Anwar G. *Muslim Spain, its history and culture.* Minneapolis: U Minnesota P, 1974.

Christians and Moors in Spain. Ed. Colin Smith, Charles Melville & Ahmad Ubaydli. 3 vols. Warminster: Aris & Phillips, 1988-92.

Delcorno, Carlo. *Giordano da Pisa e l'antica predicazione volgare.* Florence: Lettere Italiane, 1975.

xxxii BIBLIOGRAPHY

Gillespie, Vincent. "*Lukynge in haly bukes: Lectio* in some Late Medieval Spiritual Miscellanies." *Analecta Cartusiana* 106 (1984): 1-27.

Guichard, Pierre. *Structures sociales "orientales" et "occidentales" dans l'Espagne musulmane.* Paris: Mouton, 1977.

Jayyusi, Salma Khadra, ed. *The Legacy of Muslim Spain.* Leiden: E. J. Brill, 1992.

Kedar, Benjamin Z. *Crusade and Mission: European Approaches toward the Muslims.* Princeton: Princeton UP, 1984.

Khalil, Samir and Jorgen S. Nielsen, ed. *Christian Arabic Apologetics During the Abbasid Period (750-1258).* Leiden: E. J. Brill, 1994.

Leclercq, Jean. *The Love of Learning and the Desire for God: A Study of Monastic Culture.* New York: Fordham UP, 1982.

----------. "Le thème de la jonglerie dans les relations entre saint Bernard, Abélard et Pierre le Vénérable." In *Sous la Règle de Saint Benoît.* Geneva: Droz, 1982. Pp. 671-87.

Makdisi, George. *The Rise of Colleges. Institutions of Learning in Islam and the West.* Edinburgh: Edinburgh UP, 1981.

----------. *The Rise of Humanism in Classical Islam and the Christian West with Special Reference to Scholasticism.* Edinburgh: Edinburgh UP, 1990.

Matter, E. Ann. *The Voice of My Beloved: the Song of Songs in Western Medieval Christianity.* Philadelphia: U Pennsylvania P, 1990.

Menocal, María Rosa. *The Arabic Role in Medieval Literary History: A Forgotten Heritage.* Philadelphia: U Pennsylvania P, 1987.

Osheim, Duane J. "Conversion, *Conversi*, and the Christian Life in Late Medieval Tuscany." *Speculum* 58 (1983): 368-90.

Richard, Jean. *Croisés, missionnaires et voyageurs: les perspectives orientales du monde latin médiéval.* London: Variorum, 1983.

Rouse, Richard H. and Mary A. Rouse. *Preachers, Florilegia and Sermons: Studies on the* Manipulus florum *of Thomas of Ireland.* Toronto: Pontifical Institute of Mediaeval Studies, 1979.

Rubio, Luciano. "Cuatro pensadores musulmanes: Alkindi, Alfarabi, Avicena (Ibn Sina) y Algazzali (Algazel), a los dos lados de la frontera cristiano-islámica en el siglo XII y parte del XIII." *La Ciudad de Dios* 201 (1988): 323-39.

Schimmel, Annemarie. "Sufism and the Islamic Tradition." *Mysticism and Religious Traditions.* Ed. Steven T. Katz. Oxford: Oxford UP, 1983. 1Pp. 30-47.

Smalley, Beryl. *The Study of the Bible in the Middle Ages.* Notre Dame, Indiana: U Notre Dame P, 1964.

Urvoy, Dominique. "Les musulmans et l'usage de la langue arabe par les missionaires chrétiennes au moyen-age." *Traditio* 34 (1978): 416-27.

----------. *Le Monde des Ulémas andalous du V/XIe au VII/XIIIe siécle: étude sociologique.* Geneva: Droz, 1978.

Vitto, Cindy L. *The Virtuous Pagan in Middle English Literature.* Transactions of the American Philosophical Society, Vol. 79, Part 5. Philadelphia: American Philosophical Society, 1989.

Warren, Ann K. *Anchorites and Their Patrons in Medieval England.* Berkeley and Los Angeles: U California P, 1985.

Yashrutiyyah, Al-Sayyedah Fatimah. "Contemplation and Action: the Sufi Way." *Contemplation and Action in World Religions.* Ed. Yusuf Ibish and Ileana Marculescu. Seattle: U Washington P for Rothko Chapel, 1978. Pp. 212-17.

Zink, Michel. *La prédication en langue romane avant 1300.* Paris: H. Champion, 1976.

The Book of the Lover and the Beloved
Lo libre de amich e amat
Liber amici et amati

Illustration from the title page of a Latin version of Llull's *Proverbs of Ramon*
(Proverbi Ramon), printed at Venice in 1507 by Giovanni Tacuini.

Chapter 99
[201r] En qual manera blanquerna ermita feu lo libre de amich e amat
[188rb] Quomodo blaquerna librum amici et amati compilavit

1. Esdevench se un dia que lermita qui estava en Roma segons que demunt avem dit ana visitar los ermitans els recluses qui eren en Roma e atroba que en alcunes coses avien moltes de temptacions per ço cor no sabien aver la manera quis covenia a lur vida e pensa que anas a blanquerna ermita que li [201v] fees un libre qui fos de vida ermitana e que per aquel libre pogues e sabes tenir en contemplacio devocio los altres ermitans Estant un dia blanquerna en oracio aquel ermita vench a la cella de blanquerna e pregal del libre damunt dit molt cogita blanquerna en qual manera faria lo libre ni de qual materia

Quadam die contigit heremitam qui rome conversabatur prout supra dictum est ire visitando heremitas alios et inclusos qui in illis finibus morabantur invenitque eos quibusdam affligi temptationibus pro eo quia moribus et modis vite sue congruis uti nesciebant. consideravit ergo ad blaquernam heremitam proficisci ut quendam librum heremitane vite compilaret per quem posset et sciret in contemplationem continuam in ferventemque devotionem dirigire alios heremitas.

2. Estant blanquerna en aquest pensament en volentat li vench ques donas fortment a adorar e a contemplar deu per tal que en la oracio deus li demostras la manera de la materia de que ell fees lo libre Dementre que blanquerna plorava e adorava e en la sobirana stremitat de ses forçes havia puyada deus sa anima quil contemplava blanquerna se senti exit de manera per la gran frevor e devocio en que era e cogita que força damor no segueix manera com lamich ama molt fortment son amat On per aço blanquerna fo en volentat que fees libre de amich e amat lo qual amich fos feel e devot crestia el amat fos deu.

Dum autem blaquerna quadam die divinis vacaret orationibus. ecce ille heremita ad cellam blaquerne orantis accessit rogavitque eum ex predicti libri compilatione ab eo facienda. Consideravit quam plurimum blaquerna quomodo hunc librum vel ex qua materia compilaret.

Consistente blanqrna in hiis considerationibus. voluntas coegit eum applicari vehementer divinis orationibus et contemplationibus ut in ipsis deus sibi modum et materiam ostenderet e quibus faceret istum librum Cumque blanquerna deum adoraret cum lacrimis qui ad contemplandum se animam eius in summam extremitatem virium ipsius anime elevarat perpendit semetipsum de modo eiectum omne considerans quod amoris fortitudo modum non sequitur dum amatum amicus diligit vehementer. Quo circa consideravit librum amici et amati compilare itaque quod amicus esset christianus fidelissimus et devotus amatus autem esset deus

Chapter 99
How Blanquerna the Hermit made the
Book of the Lover and the Beloved

1. One day the hermit from Rome, mentioned above, went to visit the other hermits and recluses there. He found that some things caused them great temptation because they did not know how to keep the rules for their way of life. So he decided to seek out Blanquerna[1] the Hermit to make a book about the life of hermits. Such a book would give him the ability and knowledge to keep the other hermits in contemplation and devotion. One day while Blanquerna was praying, the hermit came to the cell of Blanquerna and made his request for such a book. Blanquerna pondered at length what method and what material he would use for this book.

2. As Blanquerna thought about this, the desire came over him to devote himself zealously to adoring and contemplating God so that God would show him in prayer the method and subject matter for making this book. Blanquerna cried, adoring and lifting his soul up to God, contemplating Him to the very limit of his strength. Then Blanquerna felt himself succeed thanks to this great fervor and devotion. And he realized that the power of love follows no method when the Lover fully loves his Beloved.[2] Therefore Blanquerna decided to make a book about the Lover and the Beloved, in which the Lover is the devout and faithful Christian, and the Beloved is God.[3]

---

1 The name of Llull's hero seems to have been "Blaquerna" originally, as appears in the Latin manuscript. The English translation uses the spelling "Blanquerna," which quickly replaced the original, as the Catalan manuscript shows.

2 That is, instead of creating a schematic guide for devotion, Blanquerna will create a book to foster the kind of fervent and unbounded love that joins the Lover to the Beloved.

3 Although introduced within Llull's narrative as a text for use by hermits, the *Book of the Lover and the Beloved* evidently serves all Christians.

3. Dementre considerava en esta manera blanquerna el remembra una vegada com
era apostoli li reconta .i. sserray que los serrayns an alcuns homens religiosos e enfre
los altres e aquells qui son mes preats enfre clls son unes gents qui han nom sufies E
aquells han paraules damor e exemplis abreuyats e qui donen a home gran devocio e
son paraules qui han mester espusicio e per [202r] la spusicio puja lenteniment mes a
ensus per lo qual puyament muntiplica e puja la volentat en devocio on com
blanquerna ach auda aquesta consideracio ell preposa a fer lo libre segons la manera
demunt dita e dix al ermita que sen retornas a Roma e que en breu de temps li
trametria per lo diaque lo libre de amich e amat per lo qual puria muntiplicar frevor
e devocio en los ermitans los quals volia enamorar de deu

Dum enim blaquerna hoc modo consideraret re[188va]recordatus fuit quod dum
esset papam quidam sarracenus semel retulit illi aliquos viros religiose
conversationis inter ceteros esse in regionibus sarracenorum dixitque quod hii qui
inter eos venerati sunt super omnes sunt quedam gentes nomen cuius suffias
appellatur Isti autem amorifera verba ferunt et exempla compendiosa que maximam
hominibus ingerunt devotionem. sed ut tamen intelligantur expositionibus indigent
quorum expositione ascendit intellectus magis sursum per cuius ascensum
multiplicatur et ascendit voluntas in devotionem.

Hac habita consideratione tunc blaquerna predictum opus compilare proposuit
dicens heremite qui adhuc venerat quod romam regrederetur quia per dyaconum
mitteret illi librum amici et amati per quem multiplicare posset et augere amorem
fervidum et devotionem in heremitas et iustos homines quos desideraret a divino
amore et desiderio philocapi.

Chapter 100.
Del libre de amich e amat del prolech
Incipit liber amici et amati

Blanquerna estava en consideraçio e considerava la manera segons la qual
contemplava deu e ses virtuts e con havia finida sa oracio scrivia ço en que havia
contemplat deu e aço fahia tots jorns e mudava en sa oracio novelles rahons per tal
que diversses maneres e de moltes compones lo libre de amich e amat e que [en
deleted] aquelles maneres fossen breus e que en breu temps la anima ne pogues
moltes decorrer E en la benediccio de deu blanquerna comença son libre lo qual
departi en aytants versses com ha dies en layn E cascu vers basta a tot .i. dia a
contemplar deu segons la art del libre de contemplacio

Blaquerna igitur consistebat orationibus considerans modum per quem deum cum
suis virtutibus contemplatus erat et finitis orationibus confestim scribebat ea que
contemplando deum conceperat In hiis autem vacabat semper et continue vertens in
suis orationibus novas rationes . ut hunc librum amici et amati multis et diversis
modis brevibus compilaret ob cuius brevitatem rationum anima brevi tempore
decurrere multa posset. Itaque in dei benedictione et auxilio blaquerna incepit hunc
librum quem in tot partes divisit quot dies in anno reperiuntur. Quicumque autem
secundum artem libri contemplationis deum contemplandi desiderat unus versus
huius operis ei sufficit tota die.

3. While Blanquerna was thinking in this way, he remembered how when he was pope a Saracen[4] once told him that the Muslims have various holy men. The most esteemed among these or any others are some people called sufis. They offer words of love and brief *exempla*[5] that inspire a person to great devotion. Their words require exposition, and thanks to the exposition the Intellect rises higher, which develops it and spurs the Will to devotion. After considering this, Blanquerna proposed to make a book in this manner. So he told the hermit to return to Rome and that in a little while he would send the deacon with the *Book of the Lover and the Beloved*, which would promote fervor and devotion among the hermits that he wished to make love God.

Chapter 100.
The Book of the Lover and the Beloved – Prologue

Blanquerna sat praying and considered the way in which he contemplated God and His Virtues and when he finished his prayer, he wrote down how he contemplated God; he did this every day, varying his prayer with new ideas in order to create many different kinds in the *Book of the Lover and the Beloved*, so that these would be short and the soul could discourse[6] through many in a short time. Then with divine blessing Blanquerna began his book, which he divided into as many verses as there are days in the year. Each verse suffices for contemplating God a whole day, following the method of *The Book of the Art of Contemplation*.[7]

---

4   Llull's customary term for a Muslim of any nationality.
5   In Llull's usage, this term indicates not only exemplary anecdotes, but any sort of illustrative device, including allegories, analogies, metaphors, and proverbs.
6   "Discourse" is Llull's usual term for exercise of his Great Art. His emphasis on brevity illustrates his usual preference for simpler forms of piety and knowledge.
7   Presumably the *Art of Contemplation* (an abridged version of Llull's Great Art), which follows the *Book of the Lover and the Beloved* as an appendix to the *Book of Blanquerna*. It may also refer to Llull's *Book of Contemplation on God*, an encyclopedic guide to devotion divided into 366 chapters, which he wrote during his decade of private study (1265-1275).

Començan les matafores morals
Incipiunt methaphore morales

1. Demana lamich a son amat si havia en ell nulla cosa romasa a amar El amat
respos que ço per que la amor del amich pudia mun[202v]tiplicar era a amar
Quesivit amicus ab amato utrum quicquam amandum in eo remansisset.   cui
respondens amatus dixit. Id per quod amor amici multiplicari potest in me remansit
amandum

2. ¶ les carreres per les quals lamich encercha son amat son longues perilloses
poblades de consideracions de suspirs e de plors he enluminadors damors
Vie et tramites per quos amatum inquirit amicus longi sunt nimisque periculosi
populati considerationibus suspiriis et fletibus necnon amoribus illuminati.

3. ¶ Ajustaren se molts amadors a amar .i. amat quils abundava tots damors e cascu
havia per cabal son amat e sos pensaments agradables per los quals sentien plaents
tribulacions
Multi amatores congrati fuerunt ad diligendum unum amatum qui suis replebat illos
omnes amoribus et quisque eorum eque suum ferebat in corde amatum cum gratis
cogitationibus quibus tribulationes placidas senciebant.

4. ¶ plorava lamich e dehia tro a quant de temps cessaran tenebres en lo mon per ço
que cessen les carreres infernals Ni laygua qui ha en custuma que decorrega a enjus
quant sera la ora que aja natura de pujar a ensus nils innocents quant seran mes quels
colpables
Plorabat amicus dicens quando cessabunt tenebre per seculum ut cessent tramites
infernales? vel quando erit hora ut aqua cuius nature est yma querere ascendat ad
superiora? aut quando ignocentes plures erint quam culpabiles.

5. [¶ deleted] A quant se guabara lamich que muyra per son amat nil amat quant
veura son amich languir per samor
Ha quando iactabit amicus se mori pro amato suo? aut quando videbit amatus
amicum languere suis amoribus

6. ¶ Dix lamich al amat tu qui umples lo sol de resplandor umple mon cor damor
Respos lamat sens compliment damor no foren tos ulls en plor ni tu vengut en est
loch veer ton amador
Dixit amicus amato. tu qui solem imples splendore fulgido tuis reple cor meum
amoribus. ¶ Respondit ei amatus dicens. absque amorum complemento non essent
oculi cum lacrimis nec venisset in hunc locum ad videndum amatorem tuum.

Here begin the moral metaphors

1. The Lover asked his Beloved if there was anything left in Him to love. The Beloved replied: "Whatever makes the love of a Lover grow remains to be loved in me."[8]

2. The roads where the Lover seeks his Beloved are long and dangerous, crowded with cares, longing sighs, and weeping, but illuminated with love.

3. Many Lovers joined together to love one Beloved, who filled them all with love. Each one carried his Beloved fully in his heart, with gratifying anxiety, and felt a pleasant tribulation from this.[9]

4. The Lover wept and asked: "When will darkness end in the world,[10] so that the roads to hell will close? Or the water that usually runs down, when will it have the power to rise up?[11] Or the innocent, when will they outnumber the guilty?"

5. "Ah! When will the Lover boast of dying for his Beloved? Or the Beloved, when will He see His Lover languish for His love?"[12]

6. The Lover said to the Beloved: "You who fill the sun with shining light, fill my heart with love." The Beloved replied: "Without complete love, your eyes would not weep and you would not come here to see your Beloved."[13]

---

8   Presumably God is, with regard to the human capacity for love, infinitely lovable.

9   That is, no matter how large the Church grows, God's love remains inexhaustible.

10 The shadows of unbelief or of sin that lead to damnation, a Scriptural commonplace (e.g. Psalm 107.10-11 or Isaiah 42.6-7).

11 That is, when will tearful cries reach the ears of heaven.

12 That is, when will more Christians endure martyrdom or sufferings for the sake of their Faith, a theme repeated in numerous subsequent paragraphs.

13 The Lover's plea implicitly compares God's creation of the first light (the sun) with the effects of divine illumination and grace on the soul (compare 2 Corinthians 4.6), which Llull does not always explain very precisely. The Beloved replies that the Lover's behavior already reveals the infusion of love in him.

7. ¶ Tempta lamat son amich si amava perfetament e demana li de que era la diferencia qui es enfre presencia e absençia damat Respos lamich de innorancia e ublidament e conexença e remembrament

Temptavit amatus amicum suum utrum perfecte diligeret querens ab eo que erat differentia inter presenciam et absenciam dilecti. cui respondit ignorantia et oblivio

8. ¶ Demana lamat al amich has membrança de nulla cosa que taja guardonat per ço cor me vols amar Respos hoc per ço cor enfre los trebaylls els plaers quem dones nom fas diferencia

Interrogavit amatus amicum dicens. Recordarisne aliquorum que tibi recribui quia me vis diligere? cui respondit utique [188vb] recordor quia inter labores et placita que mihi tribuis nullam differentiam mihi facis.

9. ¶ digues amich dix lamat hauras paciencia sit do[203r]bles tes languors Hoc ab quem dobles mes amors

Amice dixit amatus dic mihi habebisne pacientiam si labores tuos duplicavero? etiam si in me tuos duplices amores.

10. ¶ Dix lamat al amich sabs encara que es amor Respos si no sabs que es amor sabera que es treball tristicia e dolor

Amice dixit amatus scisne adhuc quid sit amor? cui respondit amicus si nescirem quid sit amor scirem igitur quid est labor dolor et tristicia.

11. ¶ Digueren al amich per que no respons a ton amat qui tapella Respos ja maventur a greus perills per ço que a ell pervenga e ja li parle desirant ses honors

Dixerunt quidam amico quare non respondis amato tuo qui te vocat. quibus respondit numquid gravibus periculis iam expono memetipsum ut ad eum perveniam? iamque loquor desiderando eius honores.

12. ¶ Amich foll per que destruus ta persona e despens tos diners e lexes los delits daquest mon e vas menyspreat enfre les gents Respos per honrar los honraments de mon amat qui per mes homens es desamat desonrat que honrat e amat

Amice fatue quare destruis substantiam tuam et peccuniam tuam consummis. et quare uxorem et prosperitates huius mundi derelinquis? tendens vilipensus inter homines. respondit amicus ad venerandum honores amati mei qui a pluribus vilipenditur et vituperatur quam honoretur et diligatur

13. ¶ Digues foll per amor e qual cosa es pus vesible ol amat en lamich o lamich en lamat Respos e dix quel amat es vist per amors e lamich per suspirs e per plors e treballs e dolors

Eya fatue dic quis est visibilior aut amatus in amico aut amicus in amato. Respondit dicens amatus via est per amores. amicus autem via est per suspiria. lacrimas. labores. tristicias et dolores.

7. The Beloved tested whether the Lover loved perfectly: He asked him how the presence and absence of the Beloved differed. The Lover replied: "Like ignorance and forgetting from knowledge and remembering."

8. The Beloved asked the Lover: "Do you ever remember me giving you anything as a reward for wanting to love me?" The Lover replied: "Certainly, you make no distinction between the travail and the pleasure that you give me."

9. "Tell me, Lover," asked the Beloved, "would you be as patient if I doubled your anguish?" "Of course, as long as you doubled my love."[14]

10. The Beloved said to the Lover: "Do you know what love is yet?" He replied: "If I did not know what love is, I would know what travail, sadness, and pain are."

11. They said to the Lover: "Why do you give no answer to your Beloved who calls you?" He replied: "I already risk grave danger[15] to reach Him, and already speak to Him by desiring His excellence."

12. "Foolish Lover! Why do you ruin your life, waste your money, leave your wife, ignore worldly delights, and invite scorn from people?"[16] He replied: "To honor the excellence of my Beloved, because more people ignore and dishonor than respect and love Him."

13. "Tell us, fool for love,[17] which is easier to see, the Beloved in the Lover or the Lover in the Beloved?" He answered that the Beloved is visible in love, and the Lover in longing sighs, laments, travails, and pains.

---

14 That is, love makes the Lover ignore or even enjoy his travail and sadness, a paradox repeated throughout the text.

15 Presumably the danger of martyrdom in missions among unbelievers, but perhaps also scorn and abuse from other, less devoted Christians.

16 A question perhaps posed to Llull himself, since he left his family and fortune to become an evangelist.

17 A label that Llull often applies to himself in his writings, as explained in the Introduction.

14. ¶ Encerchava lamich qui recomptas a son amat com ell per samor sostenia greus
treballs e muria e atroba son amat qui ligia en un libre on eren scrites totes les
langors que amor li donaria per son amat e tots los grats quen havia

Inquirens amicus quod referret amato suo quomodo amoribus eius graves labores
ferebat moriens. invenit eum legentem unum librum ubi scripti erant omnes langores
quos amores inferebant amico propter amatum atque omnia gaudia que propter eum
sentiebat.

15. ¶ Porta nostra dona son fill a lamich per ço que li besas son peu e que scrivis en
son libre les virtuts de nostra dona

Virgo filium suum portavit amico ad osculandum pedem ipsi filio et ad scribendum
in libro suo virtutes genitricis eius.

16. ¶ Digues auçell qui cantes est te mes en guarda de mon amat per ço quet defena
de desamor e que muntplich en tu amor Respos lauçell e quim fa cantar mas tan
solament lo senyor damor quis te a desonor desamor

O avis que cantas. numquid te posuisti in custodia amati mei ut ab odio te protegat
et multiplicet in te amorem. Respondit avis. Quis mihi dat cantare nisi solum
dominus amoris qui pro vituperio habet odium.

17. ¶ Enfre temor e sperança ha fet ostal amor on viu de pensaments e mor per
hublidaments com los fonamens [203v] son sobre los delits daquest mon

Inter spem et timorem condidit amor tabernaculum ubi vivit cogitationibus
moriturque oblivionibus quando fundamenta supersunt deliciis huius mundi.

18. ¶ Questio fo enfre los hulls e la memoria del amich cor los hulls dehien que
mellor cosa es veer lamat que membrar lo e la memoria dix que per lo
remembrament puya laygua als ulls el cor senflama damor

Questio vertebatur inter oculos et memoriam amici Quia oculi affirmando dicebant
melius esse amatum videri quam recoli. memoria vero dicebat per memorationem
ascendit aqua in oculos et cor inflammatur amore

19. ¶ Demana lamich al enteniment e a la volentat qual era pus prop a son amat e
corregueren amdos e fo ans lenteniment a son amat que la volentat

Quesivit amicus ab intellectu et voluntate quis eorum esset dilecto suo propinquior.
cucurrerunt autem ambo. sed intellectus ad amatum suum fuit cicius quam voluntas.

14. The Lover wanted to tell his Beloved that he suffered great travail and was dying for love of Him. He found his Beloved reading a book:[18] in it was written all the anguish that love for his Beloved caused him and all the joy that he felt for Him.

15. Our Lady brought her Son to the Lover so that he could kiss His foot and write in his book the virtues of Our Lady.[19]

16. "Tell me, singing bird:[20] does my Beloved watch over you to protect you from hatred and to make your love grow?" The bird replied: "And who makes me sing? Only the Lord of Love,[21] who considers hatred dishonorable."

17. Love has made its home between fear and hope, and lives on anxiety there. But it dies forgotten, when its foundations rest on worldly delights.

18. An argument arose between the eyes and the Memory of the Lover. The eyes said that it was better to see the Beloved than to remember Him, but Memory said that remembering makes the eyes water and inflames the heart with love.[22]

19. The Lover asked the Intellect and Will which was closer to his Beloved. The two ran a race, but the Intellect reached the Beloved faster than the Will.[23]

---

18 Evidently Llull's adaptation of well-known Scriptural images such as the "book of the Lord" (Isaiah 34.16) or "book of life" (Revelation 3.5). Compare paragraph 229.

19 Llull wrote several works with Marian themes, most notably the *Libre de Sancta Maria* (*Book of Saint Mary*), *Hores de Sancta Maria* (*Hours of Saint Mary*), and *Libre de "Benedicta tu in mulieribus"* (*Book of "Blessed Are You Among Women"*), all available in volume 10 of Llull's Catalan *Obres*.

20 The first appearance of this aviary interlocutor, perhaps an allusion to the "voice of the turtledove" (Song of Songs 2.12), variously interpreted in exegesis as love of God, the preaching of the apostles, the Church, secret compunctions, and human sensuality.

21 Perhaps an attempt to use the figure of the "God of Love," common in courtly literature.

22 That is, the bodily Senses must serve the Memory and other faculties of the soul.

23 The first of many paragraphs devoted to the relationship between faith and reason, a constant and problematic issue in Llull's theology, as noted in the Introduction.

20. ¶ Contrastaren se lamich e lamat e viu ho .i. altre amich qui plora tant longament tro hac feta pau e concordança enfre lamat e lamich

Obstabant inter se amicus et amatus quod videns quidam alius amicus lacrimatus fuit tanto tempore quousque pax reformata fuit et concordia inter amatum et amicum.

21. ¶ Suspirs e plors vengren a jutjament al amat e demanaren li per lo qual se sentia amat pus fortment Jutja lamat quels suspirs son pus prop a amor e los plors als hulls

Suspiria et fletus coram amato venerunt ad iudicium querentes ab eo a quo ipsorum se sentiebat ardentius amari. Iudicavit autem amatus dicens propinquiora sunt amori suspiria et fletus oculis.

22. ¶ Vench lamich beure a la font on hom qui no ama senamora com beu en la font e doblaren sos languiments e vench lamat beure a la font per ço que sobre doblement doblas a son amich ses amors en les quals li doblas langors

Venit amicus ad fontem bibitum ubi qui non diliget philocapitur quando in fontem biberit. et ei duplati fuerunt langores eius venit autem amatus ad fontem bibitum ut supra duplum duplicaret amico suo amores suos in quibus langores suos sibi duplicaret.

23. ¶ Malalte fo lamich e passavan lamat de merit lo pexia e ab amor labeurava en pasciencia lo colgava dumilitat lo vestia ab veritat lo metjava

Infirmabatur amicus. amatus autem sollicitabatur in eum cibabat eum meritis potabat eum amore. cubabat eum in paciencia. induebat eum humilitate cum veritate medicabat eum

24. ¶ Demanaren al amich on era son amat Respos vel vos en una casa pus noble que totes les altres nobilitats creades he vel vos en mes amors e en mos languiments e en mos plors

Quesitum fuit ab amico. ubi est [189ra] amatus tuus qui Respondit. ecce eum in una domo nobiliori ceteris omnibus nobilitatibus creatis. et ecce eum in meis amoribus. in meis langoribus et in fletibus meis.

25. ¶ Digueren al amich on vas vench de mon amat on vens vaig a mon amat [204r] quant tornaras estare ab mon amat quant estaras ab ton amat aytant de temps con seran en ell los meus pensaments

Quesitum fuit ab amico quo vadis? venio de amato meo. unde venis? vado ad amatum meum. quando reverteris? Cum amato meo morabor tanto tempore quanto fuerint in eo cogitationes mee.

20. The Lover and the Beloved argued. Another Lover saw this, and wept a long time, until he achieved peace and agreement between the Beloved and the Lover.[24]

21. Longing sighs and tears came to the Beloved for a judgement. They asked Him which made Him feel more strongly loved. The Beloved ruled that longing sighs were closer to love, and tears to the eyes.[25]

22. The Lover came to drink from the spring where the unloving become loving when they sip its waters.[26] And his anguish doubled. Then the Beloved came to drink at the spring, in order to double loving in the Lover again. And this doubled his anguish.

23. The Lover was ill and they called in the Beloved: He nourished him with merit; gave him love to drink; laid him in a bed of patience; dressed him with humility; and gave him medicine of truth.

24. They asked the Lover where his Beloved was. He answered: "Look for Him in a house nobler than the noblest thing in creation. Look for Him also in my love, in my anguish, and in my weeping."

25. They asked the Lover: "Where are you going?" "I come from my Beloved." "Where do you come from?" "I go to my Beloved." "When will you return?" "I will stay with my Beloved." "How long will you stay with your Beloved?" "As long as my thoughts are with Him."

---

24 Every Christian is obliged to bring other souls to God, but the emphasis on weeping gives this duty a distinctly penitential character.

25 Llull evidently regards sighs as a more direct manifestation of heart-felt love, despite his frequent references to weeping in this text.

26 An adaptation of the commonplace Scriptural image of God as a fountain for the thirsting soul (as in Psalm 42.1).

26. ¶ Cantaven los auçells lalba e despertas lamich qui es lalba e los auçells feniren lur cant el amich muri per lamat en lalba

Cantabant aves auroram. excitatus est amicus qui est aurora. aves cantus suos finierunt. mortuus est pro amato amicus in aurora.

27. ¶ Cantava lauçell en lo verger de lamat vench lamich qui dix a laucell si nons entenem per lenguatge entenam nos per amor cor en lo teu cant se representa a mos hulls mon amat

Cantabat avis in amati viridario. venit amicus dicens ei si non intelligimus nos ydiomate. intelligamus nos amore quoniam in cantibus tuis amatus meus oculis meis representatur.

28. ¶ hac son lamich qui molt havia treballat en cerchar son amat e ach paor que no ublidas son amat e plora per ço que no sadurmis ni son amat no fos absent a son remembrament

Sopnum ferebat amicus quia multum laboraverat inquirendo amatum timuitque ne obliviceretur amati sui et ploravit ne obdormiret ut amatus in cogitationibus suis non abesset.

29. ¶ Encontrarense lamich ell amat e dix lamich no cal quem parles mas fem senyal ab tos hulls qui son paraules a mon cor con te do ço quem demanes

Obviaverunt sibi amicus et amatus. dixit amicus ei. non oportet te mihi loqui sed oculis tuis signa que sunt verba cordi meo ut tibi dem que mihi queris.

30. ¶ Desobehi lamich son amat e plora lamich el amat vench murir en la gonella de son amich per ço quel amich recobras ço que havia perdut e dona li mayor do que cell que perdut havia

Amicus inobedivit amato. ploravit amicus. amatus autem venit mori in tunicam amici sui ut restauraret amico que perdiderat. dans ei maiora munera hiis que priora dedit.

31. ¶ lamat enamora lamich e nol plany de son languiment per ço que pus fortment sia amat e en lo major languiment atrop lamich plaer e reveniment

Amatus philocepit amicum nec planxit pro langore suo ut ametur fortius ut in maiori langore reperiat amicus placitum et convalescentiam.

26. Birds were singing the dawn; the Lover who is the dawn awoke.[27] The birds finished their song; the Lover died in the dawn for the Beloved.

27. A bird was singing in the garden of the Beloved.[28] The Lover came and said to the bird: "Even if we cannot communicate in words, let us communicate in love, because my Beloved appears to my eyes in your song."[29]

28. The Lover felt sleepy from working so long to find his Beloved. He was afraid that he might forget his Beloved. So he wept, to stay awake and keep his Beloved in his thoughts.

29. The Lover and the Beloved met. The Lover said to Him: "You need not talk to me; just signal me with your eyes, which speak to my heart, so that I can give you what you want."

30. The Lover disobeyed his Beloved and the Lover wept. Then the Beloved came to die in the clothes of the Lover, so that the Lover would recover what he had renounced. And the Beloved gave him greater gifts than what he had lost.[30]

31. The Beloved instills love in the Lover, but He does not regret his anguish, because it strengthens love for Him and because the Lover finds pleasure and renewal in greater anguish.[31]

---

27 Scriptural images of Christ as the "light" of salvation (as in Luke 2.32 or throughout the Gospel of John) would favor presenting the Beloved as the dawn, although medieval exegesis also identifies the dawn with the Church. Llull offers an extended comparison between the dawn and the Virgin Mary in his *Book of Saint Mary* (*Libre de Sancta Maria* in volume 10 of the Catalan *Obres*). He perhaps adapts as well the imagery of the traditional lyric dawn-song.

28 The first occurrence of this image, which broadly recalls the lyric commonplace of the *locus amoenus* as well as the "garden of the Beloved" in Song of Songs 4.16-5.1, which received exegesis interpreted variously as the Church, Sacred Scripture, and eternal life.

29 A striking use of synesthesia, although comprehensible from the medieval belief that love occurs most directly through the eyes or from understanding these as the eyes of spiritual insight.

30 A simple allegory of the doctrines of the Fall, Incarnation, Redemption and Salvation, repeated in later paragraphs.

31 Llull's most literal explanation of this paradox of love.

32. ¶ Dix lamich turmenten me los secrets de mon amat com les mies obres los revellen e cor la mia bocha los te secrets e nols descobre a les gents

Dixit amicus numquid amati mei me cruciantur arcana quando mea revelant eum opera? et quoniam os meum secrete tenet eum non revelans eum gentibus

33. ¶ les condicions damor son quel amich sia sufirent pacient humil temeros diligent confiant e que saventur a [204v] grans perills a honrar son amat e les condicions del amat son que sia vertader liberal piadors just a son amich

Conditiones amoris sunt quod amicus sit sufferens. paciens. humilis. timoratus. diligens. confidens non formidans se magnis tradere periculis ad honorandum amatum suum. conditiones autem amati sui sunt quod sit verax liberalis. pius. iustus amico suo

34. ¶ Encerchava lamich devocio en los munts en los plans per veer si era servit son amat e atroban defalliment en cascu daquests lochs e per aço cava en la terra si hi atrobaria lo compliment pus que per terra devocio a defalliment

Inquirebat amicus devotionem per montes et plana ad videndum amatum suum invenitque defectum in quolibet istorum locorum idcirco fodit terram si forte complementum inveniret in ea cum super terram careat devotio.

35. ¶ Digues aucell qui cantes damor al meu amat per quem turmenta ab amor qui ma pres a esser son servidor Respos laucell si no sostenies treballs per amor ab que amaries ton amat

Dic avis que amore concinis amato meo quare me cruciatur amore ad essendum me sibi servitorem? Respondit avis nisi amore sustineres labores et cruciamina in quo diligeres amatum tuum.

36. ¶ Consiros anava lamich en les carreres de son amat e ençepega e caech enfre spines les quals li foren semblants que fossen flors e que son lit fos damors

Considerosus ibat amicus in viis amati sui et fortitudo corruens cecidit inter spinas que sibi erant similes floribus. eiusque lectus videbatur sibi esse amoribus

37. ¶ Demanaren al amich si camiaria per altre son amat Respos e dix e qual altre es mellor ni pus noble que subiran be eternal infinit en granea poder savica amor perfeccio

Quesitum fuit ab amico utrum alterutrare vellet amatum suum per alio? amicus respondit dicens. Quis est summo bono. eternali et infinito melior et nobilior magnitudine. potestate. sapientia. amore perfectione.

32. The Lover said: "The secrets of my Beloved torment me, because my deeds reveal them, but my mouth hides them away from people."[32]

33. Love requires the Lover to be suffering, patient, humble, respectful, diligent, trusting, and willing to risk great danger to honor his Beloved. It requires the Beloved to be true, generous, merciful, and fair with His Lover.

34. The Lover looked for devotion in the mountains and on the plains, to see if his Beloved was well-served. But it was missing everywhere. So he looked for its fulfillment by digging below ground, since it was missing above ground.[33]

35. "Tell me, bird who sings of love for my Beloved, why does the One who keeps me as His servant torment me with love?" The bird answered: "If you did not suffer travails for love, how would you love your Beloved?"

36. The Lover walked lost in thought along the roads of his Beloved. He tripped and fell into some thorns, but these seemed like flowers and a bed of love to him.[34]

37. They asked the Lover if he would trade his Beloved for another. He answered: "But who else is better or nobler than the sovereign eternal good, who is infinite in greatness, power, wisdom, love, and perfection?"[35]

---

32 An interesting penitential expression of the need to match words and deeds, which Llull often presents as the ideal of all Christian evangelism.
33 That is, "on the earth." The Lover's "foolish" behavior dramatizes his moral criticism.
34 Just as the ring of thorns placed on Christ's head served as his royal "crown".
35 That is, the Lullian Divine Dignities or Absolute Principles.

38. ¶ Cantava e plorava lamich cants de son amat e dehia que pus ivaçosa cosa es amor en coratge damador que lamp en resplandor ni tro en ohiment e pus viva es aygua en plor que en ondes de mar e pus prop es suspir a amor que neu a blancor

Cantabat amicus cum fletibus cantica dilecti sui dicens. velocior est amor in amatoris animo quam fulgur in splendore et quam tonitruum in auditu magisque viva est [aqua *in margin*] in fletibus quam unda maris. propinquiora sunt etiam amori suspiria quam albedini nix.

39. ¶ Demanaren al amich per que era son amat glorios Respos per ço cor es gloria Diguerenli per que era poderos respos per ço cor es poder ni per que es savi per ço cor es saviea ni per que es amable per ço cor es amor

Interrogaverunt quidam amico quare est amatus tuus gloriosus. qui respondit. quia est gloria Rursus interrogaverunt eum. quare est potens. Quia est ipsa. [189rb] potestas et iterum. quare est amabilis? quia est ipse amor.

40. ¶ levas mati lamich e [205r] anava cerchant son amat e atroba gents qui anaven per la via e demana si havien vist son amat respongueren li dient quant fo aquella ora que son amat fo absent a sos hulls mentals Respos lamich e dix anch pus ach vist mon amat en mos pensaments no fo absent a mos hulls corporals cor totes coses vesibles me representen mon amat

Amicus mane surrexerat deambulans inquirendo amatum suum obviavitque gentibus per viam transeuntibus interrogans eas si vidissent amatum suum. Responderunt dicentes. quomodo fuit amatus tuus absens a tuis oculis mentalibus? qui respondit postquam amatum meum vidi in meis cogitationibus non a meis corporalibus oculis abfuit. quia omnia oculis visibilia eum representant.

41. ¶ Ab hulls de pensaments languiments de suspirs e de plors sguardava lamich son amat e ab hulls de gracia justicia pietat misericordia liberalitat lamat esguardava son amich el aucell cantava lo plaent sguardament demunt dit

Oculis cogitationum. languorum. suspirium. et fletuum cernebat amatum amicus. oculis autem. gratie. iusticie. pietatis. et misericordie. et liberalitatis videbat amatus amicum. avis dulces amborum speculationes concinebat.

42. ¶ les claus de les portes damor son daurades de consirers suspirs e plors el cordo de les claus es de consciencia contriccio devocio satisffacio el porter es de justicia misericordia

Claves portarum amoris deaurate sunt considerationibus. suspiriis et fletibus. et funiculus earum est conscientie. contrictionis. devotionis et satisfactionis. Ianitor autem earum est iusticie et misericordie.

38. The Lover wept and sang songs about his Beloved.[36] He said: "Love moves faster in the heart of a lover than bolts of lightning or sounds of thunder. Water falls faster in tears than in sea waves. Longing sighs belong to love more than whiteness does to snow."[37]

39. They asked the Lover why his Beloved was glorious. He answered: "Because He is glory." They said to him: "Why is He powerful?" He replied: "Because He is power." "And why is He wise?" "Because He is wisdom." "And why is He lovable?" "Because He is love."

40. The Lover got up in the morning and set out to find his Beloved. He met people walking along the way and asked them if they had seen his Beloved. They replied by asking: "When was your Beloved ever absent from your mind's eye?" The Lover replied: "Even when my thoughts no longer see my Beloved, my eyes still see Him, because everything visible reveals my Beloved to me."[38]

41. The Lover watched his Beloved with eyes full of concern, anguish, sighs, and weeping; the Beloved watched His Lover with eyes full of grace, justice, pity, mercy, and generosity. The bird sang about these pleasant sights.

42. The keys to the doors of love are gilded with cares, longing sighs, and tears. Their chain is made of conscience, contrition, devotion, and satisfaction. The doorkeeper is justice and charity.[39]

---

36 Perhaps an echo of Isaiah 5.1 or simply of the Song of Songs, understood in its broad allegorical sense as the lovesong of the church for God.

37 That is, sighs are more essential to love than whiteness is to snow, a relationship that medieval logical textbooks commonly treat as an example of an inseparable (though not strictly essential) quality of a thing.

38 Right use of the physical senses such as vision to achieve spiritual insight is fundamental to Llull's entire system.

39 Perhaps an adaptation of the commonplace image of the Senses as "portals of the soul".

43. ¶ Estava lamich a la porta de son amat ab colp damor sperança ohia lamat lo colp de son amat ab humiltat pietat paciencia caritat Obriren les portes deytat e humanitat e entrava lamich veer son amat

Ictu amoris humilitatis. pietatis pacientie et karitatis pulsabat amicus ad portam amati. portas aperuit deitas et humanitas Ingressus est amicus videre amatum.

44. ¶ Proprietat e comunitat sencontraren es mesclaren per ço que fos amistat e benvolença enfre lamich el amat

Proprietas et communitas obviaverunt sibi. commiscentes se ut inter amicum et amatum esset amicicia

45. ¶ dos son los fochs qui scalfen la amor del amich la .i. es bastit de desigs plaers cogitacions laltre es compost de temor languiment e de lagremes e de plors

Duo sunt ignes qui amorem. amici calefaciunt. unus quorum desideriis placitis. cogitationibus construitur. alius vero timore. langoribus. lacrimis et fletibus componitur.

46. ¶ Desira lamich soliditat e ana estar tot sol per ço que agues [205v] companyia de son amat ab lo qual esta tot sol enfre les gents

Desideravit amicus solitudinem. ivitque statum solus ut ab amato suo [non *deleted*] associaretur cum quo stetit solus inter gentes.

47. ¶ Estava lamich tot sol sots la ombra de un bell arbre passaren homens per aquel loch e demanaren li per que stava sol el amich respos que sol fo com los ach vists e ohits e que dabans era en companyia de son amat

Stabat amicus solus ad umbram cuiusdam arboris speciose. preterierunt homines per locum illum interrogantes ei dicentes. quare stas hic solus. Respondit eis amicus dicens quando vidi vos et audivi solus fui. qui prius ab amato meo sociabar.

48. ¶ Ab senyals damor se parlaven lamich e lamat e ab temor pensamens lagremes e plors Recomptava lamich al amat sos languiments

Signis amoriferis interloquebantur sibi ad invicem amicus et amatus. cum timore autem. cogitationibus. lacrimis et fletibus referebat amicus amato langores suos.

49. ¶ Dubta lamich que son amat no li falis a ses majors necessitats Desenamora lamat son amich ach contriccio penediment lamich en son cor el amat rete al cor del amich sperança caritat e als hulls lagremes e plors per ço que retornas amor en lamich

Dubitavit amicus amatum suum abesse sibi in maioribus necessitatibus suis. amatus amorem distulit ab amico qui contrictionem habuit et pacientiam in corde suo. amatus autem spem et karitatem in corde illius retinuit et oculis fletus et lacrimas ut reverteretur amor in amicum.

43. The Lover knocked with love and hope at the door of his Beloved. The Beloved heard the knocking by His Lover with humility, mercy, patience, and love. Divinity and humanity opened the doors, and the Lover walked in to see his Beloved.

44. The particular and the universal met and mixed,[40] so there would be friendship and good will between the Lover and the Beloved.

45. Two fires ignite love in the Lover: one is stoked with desires, pleasures, and thoughts; the other is composed of fear, anguish, tears and crying.

46. The Lover longed for solitude, so he went off to be all alone in the company of his Beloved. With Him he is all alone even among people.

47. The Lover sat all alone under the shade of a beautiful tree.[41] People passing by asked: "Why do you sit here alone?" The Lover told them: "I was alone when I saw and heard you, but before I was in the company of my Beloved."

48. The Lover and the Beloved spoke with signs of love. The Lover told the Beloved about his anguish with fear, care, tears, and weeping.

49. The Lover doubted whether his Beloved would satisfy his greatest needs: the Beloved quit loving the Lover. The Lover found contrition and repentance in his heart: the Beloved brought hope and love to the heart of the Lover and tears and weeping to his eyes, so that love would return in the Lover.

---

40   That is, Christ as an individual human was joined to humanity in general. The dependence of all particulars on real universals is an axiom of Llull's metaphysics.

41   A typical element of any *locus amoenus*, and also one of Llull's favorite symbolic devices, which he even uses to organize entire works, like his *Tree of Knowledge* (*Arbre de sciència*). Tree symbolism and organization was especially popular in Franciscan literature of his era.

50. ¶ Eguals coses son propinquitat e lunyedat enfre lamich el amat Cor enaxi com mesclament daygua e de vi se mesclen les amors del amich el amat Enaxi con calor e lugor sencadenen lurs amors e enaxi com essencia e esser sen convenen e sacosten

Equales sunt propinquitas et distantia inter amicum et amatum. nam quemadmodum commiscentur vinum et aqua commiscentur amores amati et amici et concatenantur sicut calor et lux et adherent sibi sicut esse et essentia.

51. ¶ Dix lamich a son amat en tu es mon sanament e mon languiment e on pus fortment me sanes pus creix mon languiment e on pus me languexs major sanitat me dones Respos lamat la tua amor es sagell e empremta on mostres los meus honraments a les gents

Dixit amicus ad amatum Salus mea langoresque mei in te sunt. quanto plus pro te langueo tanto plus mihi maiorem ministras salutem. cui respondit amatus dicens tuus amor sigillum est et impressio ubi meos honores revelas gentibus.

52. ¶ Vehies pendre lamich e ligar e ferir e auciure per amor de son amat Demanaven li aquells quil turmentaven on es ton amat Respos vel vos en lo muntiplicament [206r] de mes amors e en la sustentacio quem fa de mos turments

Amore amati sui se videbat amicus capi. ligari. flagellari. et occidi. tortores eius interrogabant ei dicentes. ubi est amatus tuus? qui respondit ecce eum in amorum meorum multiplicationibus et in sustentatione quam mihi tribuit tormentorum.

53. ¶ Dix lamich al amat anch no fugi nim parti de tu a amar depus que tach conegut cor en tu e per tu e ab tu fuy on que fos Respos lamat ni yo depus que tu maguist conegut e amat no tublide ni null temps no fiu contra tu engan ni falliment

Dixit amicus ad amatum nusquam a te fugii nec dereliqui diligere te postquam cognovi te quia ubicumque fui. ego in te et per te et tecum fui. respondit amatus ei postquam cognovisti et dilexisti me non oblitus sum tui et numquam fraudem nec defectum intuli tibi.

54. ¶ Anava lamich per una ciutat com a foll cantant de son amat e demanaren li les gents si avia perdut son seny Respos que son amat havia pres son voler e que ell li avia donat son enteniment per aço era li romas tan solament lo remembrament ab que remembrava son amat

Ibat amicus per unam civitatem tamquam stultus cantans de amato suo quidam [189va] de civitate interrogabant ei utrum eiectus esset a sensu. qui respondit eis. dilectus meus sustulit a me sibi velle meum. Et ego dedi ei meum intellectum. sola mihi remansit memoratio cum qua recordor illius.

50. Distance and nearness are the same between the Lover and the Beloved. Just as water mixes with wine, so the loves of the Lover and the Beloved mix. Their loves are linked just like heat and light. One belongs and goes with the other, just like essence and existence.[42]

51. The Lover said to his Beloved: "My health and my afflictions[43] come from you. Where you heal me most, my afflictions grow the most. Where you afflict me the most, you make me healthiest." The Beloved replied: "Your love is a seal and a stamp to show people my excellence."[44]

52. The Lover found himself captured, bound, beaten, and killed for love of his Beloved. His tormentors asked him: "Where is your Beloved?" He replied: "You see Him in the growth of my love and in the resistance to torment that He gives me."[45]

53. The Lover said to the Beloved: "I never ran away or stopped loving you after I met you, because wherever I was, I was in you, through you, and with you there." The Beloved replied: "And I, after you had met and loved me, never forgot, deceived, nor failed you."

54. The Lover went around the city singing like a fool about his Beloved, and people asked him if he had lost his mind. He said his Beloved had captured his Will and he had surrendered his Intellect to Him. Therefore all he had left was Memory for remembering his Beloved.

---

42   These comparisons to principles from Scholastic natural science and metaphysics constitute "necessary reasons" for Llull.

43   Literally, "anguish".

44   The Lover's love results from the Beloved's excellence, just as does the impression from a seal or stamp. Comparisons between psychological functions and the impressions of a seal often appear in Scholastic psychological literature, thanks to Aristotle's use of this analogy to describe all sensation in his treatise *On the Soul* 2.12 424a20.

45   Llull was jailed and apparently mistreated during at least two of his missionary visits to North Africa, in 1292-1293 and 1307-1308. A similar allusion to this mistreatment appears in paragraph 167.

55. ¶ Dix lamat miracle es contra amor de amich qui sadorm ublidant son amat Respos lamich e miracle es contra amor si lamat no desperta lamich pus que la desirat

Dixit amatus mirabile est contra amorem amici quare dormit amicus obliviscens dilectum suum. Respondit amicus mirabile est et contra amorem. quare dilectus amicum non excitat postquam desideravit eum.

56. ¶ puyas en lo cor del amich en les altees del amat per ço que no fos embargat a amar en labis daquest mon e com fo a lamat contemplal ab dolçor e plaer el amat baxal a aquest mon per ço quel contemplas ab tribulacions e ab languiments

Ascendit cor amici in altitudines amati ut ex abyssu mundi non impediretur diligere. cumque fuisset ad amatum contemplatus est eum cum dulcedine et placitis In mundo autem remissus est ab amato ut cum tribulationibus et langoribus contemplaretur eum.

57. ¶ Demanaren al amich quals son tes riquees Respos les pobretats que sostench per mon amat e qual es ton repos lo languiment quem dona amor e qui es ton metge la confiança que he de mon amat e qui es ton maestre respos e dix que les significances que les creatures donen de son amat

Quesiverunt ab amico que sunt divicie tue. qui respondit. paupertates quas amore dilecti mei sustineo. et iterum ubi est requies tua? respondit. In langoribus quos michi ministrat amor. et qui est medicus tuus? respondit. confidentia quam habeo in amato meo. quis est magister tuus? respondit significationes quas ex amato meo exhibent creature.

58. ¶ Cantava lauçel en un ram de fulles e de flors e lo vent menava les fulles e aportava odor deles flors demanava lamich al auçell que significava lo movi[206v]ment de les fulles ni la odor de les flors Respos les fulles signifiquen en lur moviment obediencia e la odor sufre e malanança

Cantabat avis in quodam ramo foliis et floribus redundante. quesivit amicus avi dicens quid representant foliorum motus et florum odor suavissimus. respondit avis In suo motu significant folia obedientiam odor autem florum denotat sustentationem et adversitates.

59. ¶ Anava lamich desirant son amat e encontras ab .ii. amichs qui ab amor e ab plors se saludaren e s abraçaren es besaren smortis lamich tant fortment li remembraren los .ii. amichs son amat

Ibat amicus amatum suum desiderans obviavitque duobus amicis qui cum fletu et amore se salutabant et amplexu desiderabili se osculabantur. mortificatus fuit amicus pre dulcore tam vehementer representaverunt ei amatum suum ambo amici

55. The Beloved said: "It is a miracle contrary to the love of a Lover if he falls asleep and forgets his Beloved." The Lover replied: "It is a miracle contrary to the love of the Beloved if He fails to awaken the Lover who longs for Him."[46]

56. The heart of the Lover rose up high to where the Beloved was, so it would not be bogged down in the pit of this world. When he reached the Beloved, he contemplated Him with sweet pleasure. The Beloved brought him back down to this world, so he could contemplate Him with tribulation and anguish.[47]

57. They asked the Lover: "What riches do you have?" He answered: "The poverty I suffer for my Beloved." "What relief do you get?" "The anguish love gives me." "Who is your doctor?" "The confidence I have in my Beloved." "Who is your teacher?" He answered: "The signs of my Beloved given by creatures."

58. The bird sang on a branch with leaves and flowers. The wind shook the leaves and carried away the fragrance from the flowers. The Lover asked the bird what the moving leaves and the fragrance from the flowers signified. He answered: "The leaves signify obedience when they move and the fragrance, suffering and misery."

59. The Lover walked along, pining for his Beloved. He met two Lovers who greeted and hugged and kissed each other with tears of love. The Lover was dazed with sweetness, because the two Lovers recalled his Beloved so strongly to him.[48]

---

46   Sleep, conventionally glossed as a metaphor for spiritual torpor or love of the world, following Scriptural passages such as Isaiah 29.8 or Lamentations 2.19. Llull also uses it in paragraphs 28, 240, 277, 340-41, and 345.

47   One of several passages that describe the mind's dual trajectory of contemplation, which oscillates between creatures (descent) and their Creator (ascent). This is in effect the fundamental dialectic of Llull's "natural theology".

48   Presumably because their loving behavior resembles God, who is constantly and completely loving. The meeting of all three lovers is perhaps an allegory of the Trinity as well.

60. ¶ Cogita lamich en la mort e ach paor tro que remembra son amat e crida a les gents qui li estaven devant ha senyors amats per ço que mort ni perills no temats a honrar mon amat

Consideravit amicus in morte fuitque perterritus usquequo dilectum suum recoluit. clamabat populo qui stabat ad spectaculum eius dicens. karissimi diligite ut mortem nec pericula abhorreatis ad honorandum amatum meum.

61. ¶ Demanaren al amich on començaren primerament ses amors Respos que en les noblees de son amat e que daquell començament senclinarien a amar si mateix e son prohisme he en desamar engan e falliment

Interrogaverunt amico dicentes ubi primo inceperunt amores tui? respondit eis in amati mei nobilitatibus nam ex hoc principio inclinavi me ad diligendum me et proximum meum mihi odiendo versucias et falsitates.

62. ¶ Digues foll sit [demanava deleted] desamava ton amat que faries respos e dix que amaria per ço que no muris con sia cosa que desamor sia mort e amor sia vida

Dic amice fatue si amatus tuus inimicaretur tibi vel odiret te quid ageres? respondit amicus dicens diligerem utique ut non morerer cum maxime odium sit mors. et amor vita.

63. ¶ Demanaren al amich quina cosa era perseverança dix que perseverança era benanança e malanança en amich perseverant en amar honrar servir son amat ab fortitudo paciencia sperança

Quesitum fuit ab amico que res esset perseverantia. respondit amatus. perseverantia est felicitas et adversitas in amico perseverante in dilectione. honorificatione. et servitio amati sui cum spe fortitudine et pacientia.

64. ¶ Dix lamich a son amat quel pagas del temps en que lavia servit comta lamat los pensaments els desigs els plors els perills els treballs que havia sostenguts son amich per samor e afigi lamat en aquell comte eternal benahuyrança e dona si mateix en paga a son amich

Dixit amicus ad amatum suum. Solve mihi pro tempore in quo tibi servivi. amatus autem computavit cogitationes. desideria. fletus. labores et pericula que amicus suus amore sui tulerat. addidit amatus illi computo eternam beatitudinem dans semetipsum amico suo pro solutione.

65. ¶ Demanaren al amich qual cosa era benanança Respos [207r] que malanança sostenguda per amor

Interrogaverunt amico quidam dicentes. quid est beatitudo. respondit. adversitas pro amore sublata.

60. The Lover meditated about death and was afraid until he remembered his Beloved. Then he cried out to the people around him: "Dear friends! Be loving, and you will fear neither death nor danger to honor my Beloved."

61. They asked the Lover where his love first began. He answered in the excellence of his Beloved. From that beginning his love extended to loving himself and his neighbor, and to rejecting deceit and deception.[49]

62. "Say, fool: if your Beloved quit loving you, what would you do?" He answered he would love in order not to die, since surely not loving is death and loving is life.

63. They asked the Lover what perseverance was. He said that perseverance was the happiness and the misery of a Lover who perseveres in loving, honoring, and serving his Beloved with fortitude, patience, and hope.

64. The Lover asked the Beloved to pay him for the time he had served Him. The Beloved counted up the cares, desires, weeping, danger, and travail His Lover had suffered for His love. Then the Beloved added eternal happiness to the total, and gave Himself in payment to His Lover.[50]

65. They asked the Lover what happiness was. He answered it was misery suffered for love.

---

49 Llull adapts Jesus's Great Commandments (Matthew 22.39) regarding the virtue of love and defines it as opposed to sin, in the manner of Scholastic moral theology.

50 Another simple allegory of the doctrine of Redemption.

66. Digues foll quina cosa es malanança membrança de les desonors qui son fetes a mon amat digne de tots honraments

dic amice fatue quid est adversitas. respondit amicus. rememoratio dedecorum illatorum amato meo omni decore digno.

67. ¶ Remirava lamich un loch en lo qual havia vist son amat e dehia a loch quim representes les belles custumes de mon amat diras a mon amat que yo sostench per sa amor treball e malanança Respos lo loch con en mi era ton amat soferia per temor mayor treball e malanança que tot los altres treballs ni les altres malanançes que amor pot donar a sos servidors

Speculabatur amicus locum unum in quo amatum suum viderat dicens loco. tu qui speciosas amati mei consuetudines mihi representas. nonne ei referes quod amore sui labores et adversitates sustineo? cui respondit locus dicens. dum amatus tuus in me fuit amore tui susti[189vb]nuit labores et persecutiones crudeliores omnibus laboribus et persecutionibus quas amor impendere possit servis eius.

68. ¶ Dehia lamich a son amat tu est tot e per tot e en tot e ab tot tu vull tot per ço que aja e sia tot mi Respos lamat nom pots aver tot sens que tu no sies de mi E dix lamich ajes me tot e yo tu tot Respos lamat que haura ton fill ton frare e ton pare dix lamich tu est tal tot que pots abundar a esser tot de cascu quis dona a tu tot

Dixit amicus ad amatum. tu es totum. et per totum et in toto et cum toto. te volo totum ut habeam totum memetipsum et sim ego ipse totus mei. respondit amatus ei me totum habere nequis nisi sis de me totus. dixit amicus ei me totum habe et ego te Respondit amatus ei. quid igitur haberent pater tuus. filius tuus et frater tuus? Inquit amicus ei. tu quidem es illud totum quod potest sufficere te esse totum uniuscuiusque qui tibi se totum tribuit.

69. ¶ Estech e perlonga lamich sos pensaments en la granea e en la durabletat de son amat e no y atroba començament ni miga ni fi e dix lamat que mesures foll Respos lamich mesur menor ab major e defalliment ab compliment e començament ab infinitat e eternitat per ço que humilitat pasciencia caritat sperança ne sie pus fortment en ma membrança

Stetit amicus et infixit cogitationes suas in altitudine et durabilitate amati sui nec invenit principium. medium et finem. Amatus ait. quid mensuras fatue? respondit amicus. minus cum maiore. defectum cum perfectione quantitatem cum infinitate et principium cum eternitate. ut humilitas paciencia. spes et karitas vehementiores sint in memoria mea

66. "Then tell us, fool: what is misery?" The Lover replied: "Remembering the dishonor shown to my Beloved, who deserves all honor."[51]

67. The Lover examined a place where he had seen his Beloved, and said to it: "Oh, place that recalls to me the beautiful ways of my Beloved! Will you tell my Beloved that I suffer travail and misery for His love?" The place replied: 'When your Beloved was here, He suffered greater travail and misery for love of you than any travail or misery that love causes for its servants."[52]

68. The Lover said to his Beloved: "You are all, for all, in all, and with all. I want all of you in order to have and be all of me." The Beloved replied: "You cannot have all of me unless you are mine." So the Lover said: "Take all of me and I will take all of you." The Beloved responded: "What will your son, your brother, and your father have?"[53] The Lover said: "You are so complete that you can be everything to everyone who is completely dedicated to you."

69. The Lover extended his thoughts about the greatness and endurance of his Beloved, but could not find any beginning, middle, or end for them. The Beloved said: "What are you measuring, fool?" The Lover replied: "I am measuring the lesser with the greater, imperfection with perfection, and beginning with infinity and eternity, so that humility, patience, love, and hope will be stronger in my Memory."[54]

---

51 Not simply the crucifixion, but the lack of respect, praise, and love shown by all unbelievers and less zealous Christians (as stated more explicitly in paragraph 99).

52 An emphasis on the magnitude of Christ's Passion, which becomes a dominant theme of popular devotion in the late Middle Ages.

53 This line applies especially to Llull, who left his family for a semi-religious vocation. This passage relies heavily on word-play regarding the Catalan term *tot* ("all," "everything," or "complete"), a device also employed extensively in paragraphs 296-311.

54 Lullian Relative Principles like Beginning, Middle, and End relate the creator to creatures as the greater to the lesser, the perfect to the imperfect, and so forth.

70. ¶ les vies damor son longues e breus per ço cor amor es clara pura nedea vera subtil simple forts diligent lugorosa abundosa de novells pensaments e de antichs remembraments

Vie amoris breves et longe sunt quia amor est clarus purus. mundus. verus. subtilis. simplex. fortis. diligens. fulgidus. repletivus novis cogitationibus et memorationibus antiquis.

71. ¶ demanaren a lamich quals son los fruyts damor Respos plaers cogitaments [207v] desigs suspirs ansies treballs perills turments languiments sens aytals fruits nos lexa amor tochar a sos servidors

Quesiverunt quidam ab amico qui sunt fructus amoris. respondit amicus. placita cogitationes. desideria. labores. pericula tormenta et langores. nam absque hiis fructibus amor a suis servitoribus se tangi non permittit.

72. ¶ Estaven moltes gents denant lamich quis clamava de son amat com no crexia ses amors e clamavas damor com li donava treballs ni dolors Escusas lamat dient que los treballs don acusava amor eren muntiplicaments damors

Stabat gens plurima coram amico conquerente de amato suo quia ei amores suos non augebat. dum prestabat ei labores et dolores. amatus autem excusabat se dicens quod labores et dolores unde incusabat amorem erant amorum multiplicatio.

73. ¶ digues foll com no parles ni que es ço en que estas embarbesclat consiros respos en les bellees de mon amat e en lo resemblament de les benananças e de les dolors que maduen em donen amors

Dic fatue quare non loqueris. quis es in quo stas stupefactus considerans? respondit amicus in pulcritudinibus amati mei et in consimilitudinibus beatitudinum et dolorum que me deducunt et conferunt mihi pro amoribus.

74. ¶ digues foil qual cosa fo enans o ton cor o amor Respos e dix que en un temps foren son cor e amor cor si no ho fossen lo cor no fora creat a amar ni amor no fora creada a cogitar

Dic fatue quid prius fuit vel cor tuum vel amor? respondit amicus dicens. cor et amor mei in eodem tempore fuerunt. alioquin cor non esset creatum ad amandum. nec amor ad cogitandum.

75. ¶ demanaren al foll on comença enans sa amor o en los secrets de son amat o en revelar los a les gents Respos e dix que amor no y fa null departiment com es en son compliment cor ab secret te lamich secret los secrets de son amat e ab secret los revela e ab revelacio los te secrets

Interrogaverunt quidam amico dicentes. fatue ubi incepit prius amor tuus aut in secretis amati tui. aut in revelatione eorum gentibus? respondit amicus. amor nullam facit in hoc divisionem dum est in perfeccione sua quia cum secreto tenet amicus secrete secreta dilecti sui et cum secreto revelat ea et cum revelatione secrete tenet ea.

70. The ways of love are long and short, because love is clear, pure, clean, true, subtle, simple, strong, diligent, shining, and full of new cares and old memories.

71. They asked the Lover what the fruits of love were. He answered: "Pleasure, meditation, desire, sighs, anxiety, travail, danger, torment, and anguish: love does not allow its servants to touch it without these fruits."

72. The Lover criticized his Beloved in front of a great crowd for not increasing his love. He also criticized love for causing him travail and pain. The Beloved defended Himself saying that the travail and pain he criticized in love were additional love.

73. "Say, fool, why don't you speak? What are you pondering so perplexed?" He answered: "The beauty of my Beloved and the resemblance between the pleasures and pains that love brings and gives me."

74. "Say fool, which came first, your heart or love?" He answered that his heart and love came together; otherwise, the heart would not have been created for loving or love for meditation.[55]

75. They asked the fool where his love first began, whether in the secrets of his Beloved or in revealing them to people. He answered that love makes no such distinction when it is perfect: the Lover secretly keeps the secrets of his Beloved secret. He reveals them secretly, and by revealing them keeps them secret.[56]

---

55 Or, in Scholastic terms, love is the proper act of the heart and therefore pertains to its essential nature.

56 The "secrets" mentioned here and in other paragraphs perhaps recall the commonplace sufi theme of the secrets revealed by God to "God's friends" (the sufis), although these typically involve esoteric spiritual knowledge, rather than the special affective relationship suggested by Llull.

76. ¶ Secret damor sens revelacio dona passio e languiment e revelar amor dona temor per frevor e per aço lamich en totes maneres ha languiment

Amoris secreta sine revelatione passionem inferunt et langores. revelatio autem amoris timorem concitat per magnum fervorem. Ideo ab utraque parte convertuntur langores super amicum.

77. ¶ Apella amor sos amadors e dix los que li demanassen los dons que li eren pus desirables e pus plaents e ells demanaren a amor quels vestis els ornas de sos afayçonaments per ço quen fossen a lamat pus agradables

Convocavit amor amatores suos dicens petite a me dona magis desiderabilia magisque placida vobis. qui petiverunt dicentes orna et indue nos pulchritudinibus ut amato magis amabiles efficiamur.

78. ¶ Crida lamich en alt a les gents e dix que amor los manava que amasen en anant en seent en vetlant en durment en parlant en [208r] callant en comprant en venent en plorant en rient en plaer en languiment en guanyant en perdent e en qualsque coses feessen en totes amassen cor damor navien manament

Clamabat amicus populo dicens. amor iubet vos amare eundo et sedendo. vigilando et dormiendo. loquendo et silendo. plorando et ridendo. gaudendo et tristando. convalescendo et languendo [190ra] vendendo et emendo lucrando et perdendo et in quibuscumque agitis diligite iussu amoris.

79. ¶ digues foll quant vench en tu amor Respos en aquell temps que menrequi em pobla mon cor de pensaments desirers suspirs languiments e abunda mos hulls de lagremes e de plors [¶ inserted] que taporta amor belles fayçons honráments e valors de mon amat En que vengren en membrança e en enteniment ab quells reevist ab caritat sperança ab quels guardes ab justicia prudencia fortitudo temprança

Dic fatue quando advenit in te amor? amicus respondit. in illo tempore quando me ditavit amor. replevit cor meum cogitationibus. desideriis. suspiriis. langoribus. rigans oculos meos ubertate lacrimarum cum fletibus Quid attulit amor tibi? formosos aspectus honorificationes et valores amati mei. In quid venerunt ista. in memoria et in intellectu. Cum quibus recepisti ea? cum spe et karitate. Cum quibus custodibus. cum iusticia prudentia fortitudine et temperantia.

80. ¶ Cantava lamat e dehia que poch sabia lamich de amor si avia vergonya de loar son amat ni sil temia honrar en aquells lochs on pus fortment es desonrat e poch sab damar qui senuya de malenança ni quis desespera de son amat no fa concordança damor sperança

Cantabat amatus dicens. amicus pauca scit amoris. si amatum laudare verecundetur et si eum venerari formidet ubi plus vituperatur. modicum enim scit diligere quem fastidit adversitas. Et qui desperat ab amato suo ignorat concordantiam spe et amoris.

76. A secret love left unrevealed causes anguish and suffering. Revealing love causes fear of its fervor. So the Lover is left languishing either way.

77. Love called together its Lovers and said: "Ask me for the gifts most desirable and pleasing to you." They asked love to dress and adorn them in its beauty,[57] so they would be more pleasing to the Beloved.

78. The Lover called out loud to people. He told them that love commanded them to be loving when walking, sitting, waking, sleeping, speaking, keeping silent, buying, selling, weeping, laughing, enjoying, languishing, gaining, and losing. Whatever they did, they must do it with love, because love commanded them.

79. "Say, fool, when did love come to you?" He replied: "At the moment I enriched and crowded my heart with cares, desires, sighs, and anguish and my eyes overflowed with tears and weeping." "What did love bring you?" "The beautiful appearance, excellence, and worthiness of my Beloved." "Where did they enter?" "Through remembering and understanding." "How did you receive them?" "With hope and love." "How do you keep them?" "With justice, prudence, fortitude, and temperance."[58]

80. The Lover sang a song. He said a Lover knew little about love if he felt ashamed to praise his Beloved or if he was afraid to honor Him in the places where people dishonor Him most. He knows little about loving if he becomes angry about misery. And he ignores the accord between love and hope if he despairs of his Beloved.

---

57   Probably the virtues and good works fostered by love.
58   This paragraph evidently refers to the three theological virtues (faith, hope, and love) and four cardinal virtues (justice, prudence, fortitude, and temperance), although it is not clear which element corresponds to faith.

81. ¶ trames letres lamich a son amat en les quals li dix si havia altre amador qui li ajudas a portar e a soferir los greus afanys que soste per samor el amat rescrisch a son amich dient que no ha ab que faça ves ell injuria ni falliment

Descripsit amato amicus diçens [utrum *in margin*] sibi alium fecerat amatorem qui portare iuvaret eum et sufferre graves sustentationes quas amore sui sustinebat. rescripsit amatus ei. dicens quod omne deerat per quod inferret ei iniuriam et defectum.

82. ¶ demanaren al amat de la amor de son amich Respos que la amor de son amich es mesclament de plaer e malenança e de temor ardiment

Interrogaverunt quidam amato dicentes Quid est amor amici tui? Respondit amatus. comixtio placitorum et adversitatum. timor et audacia

83. demanaren a lamich de la amor del amat Respos que la amor de son amat es influencia de infinida bonea eternitat poder saviea caritat perfeccio la qual [208v] influencia ha lamat a lamich
Rursus interrogaverunt amico. quis est amor amati tui? Respondit amicus. Influentia infinite bonitatis. eternitatis. potestatis. sapientie. karitatis. perfectionis quam influentiam habet amatus amico

84. ¶ Digues foll quina cosa es meravella Respos amar mes les coses absents que les presents e amar mes les coses vesibles corroptibles que les invisibles incorruptibles

Dic amice fatue quid est mirabile? qui respondit. diligere plus absentia quam presentia. et diligere plus visibilia corruptibilia quam invisibilia incorruptibilia.

85. ¶ Encerchava lamich son amat e atroba un home qui muria sens amor e dix que gran dampnatge era dome qui muria a nulla mort sens amor E per aço dix lamich al home qui muria digues per que mors sens amor Respos per ço cor sens amor vivia

Ibat amicus querens amatum suum invenitque quendam hominem absque amore morientem. dicens dampnum est hominem absque amore ulla morte mori. Iterum inquit ei. quare sine amore moreris? qui respondit. quia vixi sine amore.

86. ¶ Demana lamich a son amat qual cosa era major o amor o amar Respos lamat e dix que en creatura amor es larbre e amar es lo fruyt els treballs els languiments son les flors e les fulles e en deu amor e amar son una cosa matexa sens negun treball languiment

Quesivit amicus ab amato suo dicens quid maius est aut amor aut amare? Respondit amatus ei dicens. In creatura est amor arbor. amare vero fructus eius est labores et langores sunt eius flores et folia In Deo autem sunt amor et amare unum idem. sine omni labore et langore.

81. The Lover wrote to his Beloved, asking whether He had another Lover who could help him bear and suffer the great travail that he endured for His love. But the Beloved wrote back and told His Lover there was nothing that would injure or harm him.[59]

82. They asked the Beloved about the love of His Lover. He replied that his love mixes pleasure and misery or fear and daring.

83. Then they asked the Lover: "What is the love of your Beloved?" He replied: "The influence of infinite goodness, eternity, power, wisdom, love, and perfection.[60] This is the influence that the Beloved has on the Lover."

84. "Fool! Tell us something incredible!" He replied: "Loving things that are absent more than things that are present; loving visible things that change more than invisible things that never change."[61]

85. The Lover was looking for his Beloved. He came across a man who was dying without love. He said it was a great curse for someone to face death without love. So the Lover said to the dying man: "Tell me, why are you dying without love?" He answered: "Because I lived without love."

86. The Lover asked the Beloved whether love or loving was greater. The Beloved answered that in creatures, love is the tree, loving the fruit, travail the flowers, and anguish the leaves. But in God, love and loving are all one thing without any travail or anguish.[62]

---

59 The exchange of secret messages, a common device in courtly literature, provides a simple allegory for spiritual communication.

60 Like the Lullian Divine Dignities or Absolute Principles, which infuse all creation.

61 That is, the human, ephemeral experience of this world versus the divine, eternal verities of heaven.

62 Another use of tree symbolism to present a lesson in theological metaphysics: an operation such as love manifests itself diversely and often imperfectly (that is, with "travail") in creatures, but is wholly one and perfect in the Creator.

87. ¶ Estava lamat en languiments e en tristicia per sobre abundancia de pensaments e trames prechs a son amat que li trametes .i. libre on fossen scrites ses fayçons per ço que li donas alcun remey lamat trames aquell libre a son amich e doblaren al amich sos trebaylls e sos languiments

Stabat amicus in langoribus et tristicia propter superhabundanciam cogitationum. misit preces amato suo dicens ut quendam librum sibi miteret. ubi sue speciositates scripte forent. ut remedium aliquod prestaret ei. Amatus librum illum misit amico suo. duplicesque sentiit amicus labores suos et langores.

88. ¶ Malalte fo lamich per amor e entral veer un metge qui muntiplica ses langors e sos pensaments e sanat fo lamich en aquella hora

Infirmabatur amicus propter amorem. medicus quidam ingressus ad eum qui suos langores et cogitationes multiplicavit. sanatus fuit amicus in illa hora.

89. ¶ Apartaren se lamich e amor e tenien solaç del amat e representas lamat plora lamich e esvaneis amor en lesmortiment [209r] del amich Reviscola lamat son amich com li remembra ses fayçons

Traxerunt se ad partem amicus et amor de amato gerentes solatia. amatus se representavit. ploravit amicus amor evanuit in mortificatione amici. Amatus vivificavit amicum dum [de in margin] pulchritudine sua memorem fecit eum.

90. ¶ dehia lamich al amat que per moltes carreres venia a son cor es representava a sos hulls e per molts noms lo nomenava sa paraula mas la amor ab que lavidava ell mortificava no era mas .i. tant solament

Dixit amicus ad amatum. per multas vias venis ad cor meum et [190rb] representaris oculis meis. multisque nominibus te nominat verbum meum. unicus autem est amor cum quo me mortificas et auxiliaris mihi.

91. ¶ Entresenyas lamat a son amich de vermells e novells vestiments e esten sos braços per ço que labraç e enclina son cap per ço que li do un besar e esta en alt per ço quel puscha atrobar

Intersignavit se amatus amico suo. novis et rubeis vestimentis. et expansit brachia ut amplectaretur eum. inclinavitque caput ut unum porrigeret ei osculum stetit etiam in alto ut inveniri posset.

92. ¶ Absentas lamat a son amich encerchava lamich son amat ab memoria e ab enteniment per ço quel pugues amar Atroba lamich son amat demana li on havia estat Respos en la absencia de ton remembrament e en la innorancia de ta intelligencia

Absentavit se amatus amico suo. amicus inquirebat amatum suum cum memoria et intellectu ut posset eum diligere invenitque eum querens ubi fuerat Respondit amatus in absentia tue recolentie et in ignorantia intelligentie tue.

87. The Lover[63] languished in sadness, overwhelmed with many cares. So he begged his Beloved to send him a remedy — a book explaining His beauty. The Beloved sent His Lover that book and the Lover felt his travail and anguish double.

88. The Lover was sick with love. A doctor came to see him, and increased his anguish and cares. From that moment the Lover was cured.[64]

89. The Lover and love withdrew, taking pleasure from the Beloved. The Beloved showed himself. The Lover wept and love vanished as the Lover fainted. The Beloved revived His Lover when He recalled His beauty to him.

90. The Lover told the Beloved: "You enter my heart and appear to my eyes in many ways, and my words name you with many names, but you weaken and strengthen me with one love alone."[65]

91. The Beloved showed Himself in new crimson clothes to the Lover, opened His arms to embrace him, and lowered His head to kiss him. Yet He remained on high, so that he could find Him.[66]

92. The Beloved withdrew from His Lover. The Lover sought his Beloved with Memory and Intellect, in order to love Him. The Lover found his Beloved and asked Him where He had been. He replied: "In your wandering remembrance and inattentive understanding."[67]

---

63   The Catalan text mistakenly says "Beloved."
64   Paragraphs 87 and 88 illustrate the paradoxical effects of remedies for love, applied to the mind and body, respectively.
65   Another reference to the diversity of creatures that manifest the one Creator.
66   A description of Christ crucified, wearing red (the color of martyrs), as the higher ideal that every Christian seeks.
67   Elsewhere in his oeuvre, Llull characterizes thus the faith of unbelievers and skeptical Christians, whose minds require a strong system (such as his own Great Art) to guide them.

93. ¶ Digues foll has vergonya de les gents con te veen plorar per ton amat Respos que vergonya sens peccat es per defalliment damor qui no sab amar

Dic amice fatue numquid dedecus pateris dum flens pro amato tuo specularis a gentibus? respondit amicus. verecundia sine peccato provenit ex defectu amoris qui diligere nescit.

94. ¶ Sembrava lamat en lo cor del amich desigs suspirs virtuts e amors Regava lamich les sements ab lagremes e ab plors

Seminabat amatus in cor amici sui desideria. suspiria. virtutes et amores. rigabat amicus hec semina lacrimis cum fletibus.

95. Sembrava lamat en lo cors del amich treballs tribulacions languiments Sanava lamich son cors ab sperança devocio paciencia consolacions
Seminabat amatus in corpus amici labores tribulationes et langores. sanabat amicus corpus suum spe. devotione et consolationibus

96. ¶ A una gran festa tench lamat gran cort de molts honrats barons e feu grans convits e grans dons ˙Vench lamich a aquella cort dix li lamat qui ta apellat a venir a ma cort Respos lamich necessitat e amors man fet venir veer tes fayçons [209v] e tos capteniments

Quodam festo maximo tenuit amatus curiam magnam cum multis baronibus inclitis fecitque convitationes nobiles dans maxima munera Accessit amicus ad curiam et ingressus est. Inquit amatus ei amice ad quid venisti. quis vocavit te ad curiam? respondit amicus amor et necessitas me venire compellunt ut videam decorum pulchritudinis tue.

97. ¶ demanaren al amich de qui era Respos damor de que est damor qui ta engenrat amor on nasquist en amor qui ta nudrit amor de que vius damor com has nom amor don vens damor on vas a amor on estas en amor [¶ *inserted*] has altra cosa mas amor Respos hoc colpes e torts contra mon amat ha en ton amat perdo Dix lamich que en son amat era misericordia e justicia E per aço era son ostal enfre temor he sperança

Dixerunt quidam amico. cuius es? qui respondit. amoris. de quo es. de amore. quis igitur te generavit? amor. Ubi natus es? in amore. quis te nutrivit? amor. De quo vivis? de amore. quo vadis? ad amorem. ubi manes? in amore. habesne aliquid preter amorem? Ait illis utique culpas et iniurias erga amatum meum. nonne est in amato tuo venia? qui respondit. In amato meo sunt misericordia et iusticia. ideo tabernaculum meum est inter timorem et spem.

98. ¶ Absentas lamat al amich e encercal lamich ab sos pensaments e demanaval a les gents ab lenguatge damor

Absentavit se amatus ab amico.˙ Amicus suis cogitationibus perscrutabatur eum. a gentibus querens eum amoris ydiomate.

93. "Say, fool, are you ashamed when people see you weeping for your Beloved?" The Lover replied: "Shame without sin comes from lack of love, which knows nothing of loving."[68]

94. The Beloved sowed desires, longing sighs, virtues, and love in the heart of the Lover. The Lover watered the seeds with tears and weeping.

95. The Beloved sowed travail, tribulation, and anguish in the body of the Lover. The Lover healed his body with hope, devotion, patience, and consolation.[69]

96. On a great holiday the Beloved held a great court for many noble lords. He sent out great invitations and gave great gifts. The Lover came to that court and the Beloved said to him: "Why did you come? Who summoned you to my court?" The Lover replied: "Necessity and love made me come, to behold your lovely beauty."[70]

97. They asked the Lover where he was from. He replied: "From love." "What are you made of?" "Love." "Who conceived you?" "Love." "Where were you born?" "In love." "Who raised you?" "Love." "What do you live on?" "Love." "What is your name?" "Love." "Where do you come from?" "Love." "Where are you going?" "To love." "Where are you?" "In love." "Do you have anything besides love?" He replied: "Yes, sins and and offenses against my Beloved." "Does your Beloved pardon you?" The Lover said there was mercy and justice in his Beloved and so he found shelter between fear and hope.

98. The Beloved went away from the Lover. So the Lover sought Him in his thoughts, and asked people about Him with the language of love.

---

68   That is, the true Lover is ashamed of his sin, not of his love.
69   Paragraphs 94 and 95 offer another illustration of love's effects on the mind and body, respectively.
70   This example evidently contrasts the Lover who attends his lord from love alone with the great nobles who only respond to invitations and gifts.

99. [¶ *inserted*] Atroba lamich son amat qui estava menyspreat enfre les gents e dix al amat que gran injuria era feta a sos honraments Respos lamat e dix que ell prenia desonor per fretura de fervents e devots amadors plora lamich e multiplicaren ses dolors aconsolaval lamat mostrant li sos capteniments
Invenit amicus amatum stantem neglectum et vituperatum inter gentes. Inquit amicus ei. Iniuria quidem non minima infertur honoribus tuis. cui respondit amatus dicens. Adest enim mihi dedecus propter indigentiam devotorum et ferventium amatorum ploravit amicus. multiplices sunt dolores eius. Amatus autem consolabatur eum pandens ei pulcritudinem suam.

100. ¶ lo lum de la cambra del amat vench inluminar la cambra del amich per ço quen gitas tenebres e que la umplis de plaers e de langors e de pensaments e lamich gita de sa cambra totes coses per ço que hi cabes son amat
Lux thalami amati venit ad illuminandum amici thalamum. ut ab eo fugaret tenebras. replens eum placitis. langoribus et cogitationibus. amicus omnia deiecit a talamo ut amatus suus in eum reciperetur.

101. ¶ Demanaren al amich quyn senyal fahia son amat en son gamphano respos que de home mort digueren li per que fahia aytal senyal Respos per ço cor fo ome mort crucificat e per ço que aquells quis guaben que son sos amadors se[210r]guesquen son sclau
Interrogaverunt quidam amico dicentes. Quid signum gerit amatus tuus in vexillo suo? respondit amicus. Signum hominis mortui? qui dixerunt, quare gerit signum tale? ait illis quia fuit homo mortuus crucifixus ut qui se iactant servos eius esse sequantur vestigia eius.

102. ¶ Vench lamat albergar al ostal de son amich e lo mayordome demana li hostalatge mas lamich dix que son amat devia esser albergat en perdo
Venit amatus ad hospitandum in tabernaculo amici sui [190va] minister domus hospitagium quesivit ab eo solvi. amicus dixit. amatus meus libere hospitari debet.

103. Acompararen se memoria e volentat e puyaren en lo munt del amat per ço quel enteniment sexalças e la amor se doblas en amar lamat
Memoria et voluntas associaverunt se ascendentes in monte amati ut exaltaretur intellectus et duplicaretur amor ad diligendum amatum.

104. ¶ Tots jorns son suspirs e plors misatges enfre lamich el amat per ço que sia enframdos solaç companyia e amistat e benuolença
Fletus et suspiria semper sunt nuncii inter amicum et amatum ut sint inter ambos solatia. concomitantia. amicicia et benivolentia.

99. The Lover found that people scorned his Beloved, so he told his Beloved: "This is a great insult to your dignity." The Beloved answered: "It dishonors me to lack fervent and devout Lovers." The Lover wept and his pain increased, but the Beloved consoled him by revealing His beauty.[71]

100. The light from the room of the Beloved shined into the room of the Lover, relieving its darkness and filling it with pleasure, anguish, and cares. The Lover threw everything out of his room in order to welcome the Beloved there.[72]

101. They asked the Lover what symbol his Beloved displayed on His flag. He said: "A dead man." They asked: "Why this symbol?" He replied: "Because He was a dead man, when crucified, and so that all who boast of being His Lovers would follow in His footsteps."

102. The Beloved came for lodging to the inn[73] of the Lover, and the innkeeper asked Him to pay for His stay. But the Lover said his Beloved should lodge there for free.

103. Memory and Will together climbed the mountain of the Beloved,[74] so that the Intellect would rise up and love would double from loving the Beloved.

104. Every day sighs and tears carry messages between the Lover and the Beloved, so that solace, companionship, friendship, and goodwill will exist between them.[75]

---

71 Llull's concern for this dishonor coincides with the penitential theme that the misconduct of contemporary sinners is prolonging Christ's Passion noted in the Introduction.

72 A conventional image for the innermost recesses of the soul. The Latin term *thalamus* especially suggests the imagery of "bridal mysticism" developed in commentaries on the Song of Songs. The Lover expels all mundane thoughts in order to concentrate on contemplation of the Beloved. The young Blanquerna describes himself as a "room" (*càmbra*) where God dwells in chapter 5.3 of the *Book of the Blanquerna*.

73 Literally "hostal" in the Catalan text and "tabernacle" in the Latin version. Blanquerna calls himself a "tabernacle" for God in chapter 5.3 of the *Book of Blanquerna*.

74 An image often used by Llull to describe how the mind's faculties aid each other in knowing, loving, and remembering God.

75 Paragraphs 104 through 108 evidently use terms--such as companionship, goodwill, sending gifts, endowments, wealth, liberality, and honors--that recall courtly culture and especially define the relationship of Lover to Beloved as a kind of bond between vassal and Lord.

105. ¶ Enyorava lamich son amat e trames li sos pensaments per ço que li aportasen de son amat la benanança en la qual lavia tengut longament
desiderabat enim amicus amatum suum mitens ei cogitaciones suas ut afferent ei beatitudinem amati sui. in qua amatus eum diu tenuerat.

106. ¶ benefici dona lamat a son amich de plors suspirs langors pensaments e dolors ab lo qual benefici servia lamich son amat

Amatus amico suo fletuum suspiriorum. langorum cogitationum et dolorum contulit beneficia cum quibus serviebat amato amicus.

107. ¶ prega lamich son amat que li donas larguea pau honrament en est mon el amat demostra ses fayçons al remembrament el enteniment del amich e donas a la volentat per object

Oravit amicus amatum dicens. concede mihi amate mi meis temporibus largitatem. pacem. et honorem in hoc seculo. amatus ostendit faciem suam memorie et intellectui amici concedens se voluntati eius pro obiecto.

108. ¶ demanaren al amich en que esta honrament Respos que en entendre e amar son amat e demanaren li en que esta desonor Respos que en ublidar desamar son amat

Interrogaverunt quidam amicum dicentes in quo existit honor? Respondit amicus in intelligendo et amando amatum meum. et in quo existit dedecus in obliviscendo amare amatum meum.

109. ¶ Turmentaven amor tro que li hac dit que tu eres present als meus turments e adoncs amor afluxa mos languiments e tu per guardo muntipliquest amor quim dobla mos turments

Dixit amicus ad amatum. amor me cruciabatur usquequo dixi te esse presentem suppliciis meis. tunc amor langores meos relaxavit tu autem propter premia multiplicasti amorem qui mea cruciamina duplicavit.

110. ¶ Encontre en la via damor amador qui no parlava ab plors magres fayçons languiments acusava amor e blas[210v]mava Escusavas amor ab leyaltat sperança paciencia devocio fortitudo temprança benanança E per aço blasme lamador qui damor se clamava pus que tan nobles dons li donava amor

In via amoris obviavit amicus amatori non loquenti. cum fletibus. facie macra. et langoribus accusabat amorem increpans eum. amor autem se excusabat cum legalitate. spe. pacientia. devotione. fortitudine temperantia et beatitudine. idcirco redarguit amatorem cum tanta munera inclita prebuit amor illi.

105. The Lover missed his Beloved and sent his thoughts to Him, to bring from his Beloved the happiness that the Beloved had provided to him for so long.

106. The Beloved endowed the Lover with tears, sighs, suffering, anguish, and pain. With this endowment the Lover served the Beloved.

107. The Lover begged his Beloved to give him wealth, peace, and honors in this world. The Beloved revealed His features to the Memory and Intellect of the Lover, and gave Himself as an object for his Will.[76]

108. They asked the Lover: "What does honor consist of?" He answered: "Understanding and loving the Beloved." Then they asked him: "What does dishonor consist of?" He answered: "Forgetting and not loving the Beloved."

109. The Lover said to the Beloved: "Love tormented me until I told it that you were present in my torments. Then love lessened my anguish. But you increased love as a reward, and that doubled my torment."

110. On the path of love I met a Lover who did not speak. With tears, weary looks, and anguish he blamed and criticized love. Love defended itself with loyalty, hope, patience, devotion, fortitude, temperance, and happiness. So I criticized the Lover who railed against love, since love gave him so many noble gifts.[77]

---

76 That is, the Beloved is simultaneously an object of attention for all three of the Lover's mental faculties.

77 The Latin version lacks the phrase "who railed against love", which appears in the Catalan text but is difficult to reconcile with the initial statement that this other Lover does not speak. Perhaps these lines form an oxymoron like "eloquent silence". The other Lover's failure to speak does reflect well his ingratitude and failure to appreciate the joy of love's pains (neatly summarized in paragraph 111).

111.   ¶ Cantava lamich e dehia o con gran malanança es amor   A con gran benauyrança es amar mon amat qui ama sos amadors ab infinida amor eternal complida en tots acabaments

Cantabat amicus dicens. ha quantus morbus est amor. ha quam magna beatitudo est amare amatum meum qui amat amantes se cum amore infinito eternali et completo in omnibus perfectionibus.

112.   ¶ Anava lamich en una terra estranya on cuydava atrobar son amat e en la via asaltejaren lo .ii. leons paor hac de mort lamich per ço cor desirava viure per servir son amat e trames son remembrament a son amat per ço que amor fos a sos trespassaments per la qual amor mills pogues sostenir la mort   Dementre quel amich remembrava lamat los leons vengren humilment al amich al qual leparen les lagremes de sos hulls qui ploraven e les mans els peus li besaren el amich ana en pau encerquar son amat

Ibat amicus in terram alienam ubi sperabat amatum suum invenire. confluxerunt ei duo leones in via. formidavit mortem amicus quia vivere desiderabat ut serviret amato suo ad hoc quod amor preesset eius obitui ut per eum dulcius mortis conflictum sustineret. dum autem amicus amati sui recordaretur leones humiliter accesserunt ad amicum cui linxerunt lacrimas que cum fletu manabant ab eius oculis. et manus eius et pedes osculati fuerunt. amicus ivit in pace querendo amatum.

113.   ¶ Anava lamich per munts e per plans e no pudia trobar portal on pugues exir del carçre damor qui longament avia tengut en preso son cors e sos pensaments e tots sos pensaments e tots sos desirers e plaers

Ibat amicus per montes et plana nec poterat invenire per quod de amoris carcere posset egredi qui diutissime detenuerat captum corpus suum atque omnes eius cogitationes desideria et placita.

114.   dementre quel amich anava enaxi treballat atroba .i. ermita qui durmia pres de una bella font   ¶ desperta lamich lermita dient si avia vist en sompniant son amat Respos lermita e dix que egualment eren encarçerats los pensaments en lo carçre damor en vetlant e en durment   Molt [211r] plach al amich com havia atrobat companyo en preso e ploraren amdos cor lamat no avia molts daytals amadors dum autem iret sic laboranter invenit unum heremitam iuxta fontem amenissimum. excitavit eum amicus dicens numquam vidisti in sompnis amatum meum? cui respondit heremita dicens. concluse sunt equaliter vigilando et dormiendo omnes cogitationes mee in amoris carcere gavisus est amicus reperto socio in captivitate sua. et fleverunt ambo dulciter quia amatus copiam non habebat talium amatorum

111. The Lover sang and said: "Oh, what great misery love is! Ah, what great happiness it is to love my Beloved! He loves His Lovers with infinite and eternal love, perfectly complete."

112. The Lover travelled through a strange land, hoping to find his Beloved. On the way two lions attacked him. The Lover was afraid to die because he wished to live and serve his Beloved. He sent his Memory to his Beloved, so that he would die in love and face a sweeter struggle with death. When the Lover recalled the Beloved, the lions came humbly to the Lover. They licked the tears from his weeping eyes and kissed his hands and feet. So the Lover went in peace to find his Beloved.[78]

113. The Lover wandered over mountains and across plains, but found no exit from the prison of love. For a long time it held captive his body, his thoughts, and all his desires and pleasures.

114. While the Lover wandered in this travail, he found a hermit sleeping beside a beautiful spring. The Lover awakened the hermit and asked if he had seen his Beloved in his dreams. The hermit replied that the prison of love held his thoughts captive both when sleeping and when awake. The Lover was delighted to find a companion in prison. They both cried with joy because the Beloved had few such Lovers.[79]

---

78 In medieval exegesis, the lion is typically a symbol of pride or the devil, but also of the Jews. The reference here to travel in a "strange land" suggests missionary activity, such as Llull's own. This encounter with a lion obviously echoes the legend of Saint Jerome, whose dual reputation for study and asceticism perhaps especially attracted Llull.

79 A neat conflation of various commonplace images from diverse literary traditions: the prison of love and *locus amoenus* of love lyric, the sage hermit of romances or devotional guides, and the dreaming of allegorical visions.

115. ¶ No ha en lamat nulla cosa en quel amich no aja ansia e tribulacio nil amich no
ha cosa en si en quel amat no aja plaer e senyoria E per aço la amor del amat es en
accio e lamor del amich en languiment passio

Nichil est in amato in quo amicus anxietatem et tribulationem non sufferat. nichil
est in amico in quo amatus dominium et placita non habebat? ob hoc amor amati in
actione est. amor vero ami[190vb]ci in langoribus et passione.

116. ¶ En .i. ram cantava .i. auçell e dehia que ell daria .i. novell pensament a
amador qui lin donas dos dona lauçell lo novell pensament al amich e lamich donan
dos a lauçel per ço que aleuyas sos turments el amich senti muntiplicades ses dolors

In quodam ramo concinebat avis dicens unam novam dabo cogitationem amatori si
mihi duas cogitationes dederit. tradidit avis novam amico cogitationem. amicus
autem duas ei reddidit. ut alleviaret amicus sua supplicia. sentiit autem dolores suos
multiplicari.

117. ¶ Encontraren se lamich el amat e foren testimonis de lur encontrament saluts
abraçaments e besars e lagremes e plors e demana lamat al amich de son estament e
lamich fo embarbesclat en presencia de son amat

Amicus et amatus obviaverunt sibi. testes autem obviationis amborum fuerunt
salutes cum amplexibus et osculis et lacrime cum fletibus. quesivit amatus amico de
statu suo. stupefactus est amicus in amati presentia.

118. ¶ Contrastaren se lamich el amat e pacificaren los lurs amors e fo questio qual
amor hi mes major amistat

Adversati fuerunt inter se amicus et amatus. amores eorum [eos *inserted above
line*] pacificaverunt. Queritur cuius amor maiorem apposuit amiciciam inter eos.

119. ¶ Amava lamich tots aquells qui temien son amat e avia temor de tots aquells
qui no temien son amat E per aço fo questio qual era mayor en lamich o amor o
temor

Diligebat amicus omnes timentes amatum suum. timebatque omnes non timentes
amatum suum Queritur quis istorum maior est in amico vel amor vel timor.

120. ¶ Jurtava lamich a seguir son amat e passava per una carrera on havia .i. mal leo
qui aucchia tot home quin passava pererosament e sens devocio

Properabat amicus sequi amatum suum. transivitque per viam ubi erat leo ferus
devorans omnem hominem inherte transeuntem absque devotione.

115. Everything in the Beloved brings anxiety and tribulation to the Lover. Everything in the Lover brings pleasure and power to the Beloved. In this way the Beloved loves actively, and the Lover loves in anguish passively.[80]

116. A bird was singing on a branch. It offered a new care to any Lover who would give it two. The bird gave the new care to the Lover, and the Lover gave the bird two in order to lessen his torments. But the Lover only felt his pain increase.[81]

117. The Lover and the Beloved met. The witnesses to their meeting were greetings, embraces, kisses, tears, and weeping. The Beloved asked the Lover how he was, but the Lover was tongue-tied in the presence of his Beloved.

118. The Lover and the Beloved argued, but their love for one another reconciled them. So the question arose: whose love brought greater friendship?[82]

119. The Lover loved everyone who feared his Beloved, and was afraid of everyone who lacked fear for his Beloved. So the question arose: was love or fear greater in the Lover?

120. The Lover set out to follow his Beloved. He travelled along a road where an evil lion[83] killed anyone who passed lazily, without devotion.

121. The Lover said: "Whoever lacks fear for my Beloved must fear everything; but whoever has fear for my Beloved will be daring and ardent in everything."

---

80 Llull applies to spiritual psychology the Aristotelian distinction between activity and passivity, a fundamental division in Scholastic metaphysics.
81 Another illustration of the paradox that "less is more" in love: more concern for the beloved is less painful to the lover.
82 Paragraphs 118 and 119 construct dilemmas based on the inability to separate the elements in a relationship of mutual interaction or implication.
83 Here probably the devil who lies ready to seize the unwary.

48   LO LIBRE DE AMICH E AMAT

121. ¶ Dehia lamich qui no tem mon amat a tembre li cove totes coses e qui tem mon amat audaçia e ardiment li cove en totes tes coses

Dixit amicus qui non timet amatum meum oportet eum timere omnia praeter ipsum. qui autem timet eum audaciam habet et securitatem in omnibus.

122. ¶ Demanaren [211v] al amich de occasio e dix que occasio es plaer en penitencia e enteniment en consciencia e sperança en pasciencia e sanitat e abstinencia Consolacio en remembrament e amor en diligencia e leyaltat en vergonya e riquea en pobretat e pau en obediencia e guerra en malvolença

Interrogaverunt quidam amatum dicentes. quid est ocasio? Qui respondit. ocasio est placitum in penitentia. sanitas in abstinentia. consolatio in memoria. amor in diligentia. legalitas in verecundia. divicie in paupertate. pax in obedientia et guerra in malivolentia.

123. ¶ Enlumena amor lo nuvolat quis mes enfre lamich el amat e feu lo enaxi lugoros e resplandent com es la luna en la nit el estel en lalba e lo sol en lo dia el enteniment en la volentat e per aquell nuvolat tan luguros se parlen lamich e lamat

Illuminavit amor nubem que consurgit inter amatum et amicum fecitque eam lucidam et fulgentem tanquam luna in nocte et lucifer in aurora et tanquam sol in meridie et intellectus in voluntate. per hanc autem nubem tam fulgidam et splendentem dant inter se colloquia amatus et amicus.

124. ¶ Demanaren al hamich quals tenebres son mayors Respos que la absencia de son amat demanaren li qual es la major resplandor e dix que la presençia de son amat

Interrogaverunt quidam amicum dicentes que tenebre sunt maiores? ait illis absentia amati mei. Rursus interrogabant eum. quis est maior splendor? Qui respondit. presentia amati mei.

125. ¶ lo senyal del amat apar en lamic qui per amor es en tribulacions suspirs e plors pensaments e en menyspreament de les gents

Amati signa in amico manifestantur qui propter amorem flagitatur in tribulationibus. suspiriis et cogitationibus despectus a gentibus.

126. ¶ Escrivia lamich aquestes paraules alegres mon amat cor a ell tramet mos pensaments e per ell ploren mos hulls e sens languiments no viu ni sent ni veig ni oig ni he odoramens

Scripsit amicus hos sermones. letare amate mi. quia cogitationes meas tibi mitto? pro te fundunt oculi mei lacrimas. et sine langoribus non vivo. nec sencio nec video nec audio nec odoro.

122. They asked the Lover: "What is opportunity?"[84] He said: "Opportunity is pleasure in penitence, understanding in conscience, hope in patience, health in abstinence, consolation in remembrance, love in diligence, loyalty in shame, wealth in poverty, peace in obedience, and war in ill will."

123. Love shined into the cloud that stands between the Lover and the Beloved. It shined as bright as the moon in the night, the morning star at dawn, the sun in the day, and the Intellect in the Will. Through that bright shining cloud the Lover and the Beloved spoke.[85]

124. They asked the Lover: "Which shadows are darkest?" He replied: "The absence of my Beloved." Then they asked him: "Which light is brightest?" He said: "The presence of my Beloved."

125. The signs of the Beloved appear in the Lover: for the sake of love, he lives with tribulation, longing sighs, weeping, and cares, scorned by other people.

126. The Lover wrote these words: "Let my Beloved rejoice because I send Him my cares. My eyes weep for Him. I do not live, feel, see, hear, or smell without anguish."[86]

---

84 Understood by Llull as a Scholastic metaphysical principle that indicates a closer relation of cause and effect than sheer chance would involve.
85 Paragraphs 123 and 124 offer commonplace images regarding divine illumination of the human soul. The "cloud" especially recalls the often-repeated fog imagery of Job 3.5, usually interpreted in medieval exegesis as representing error, confusion, or penitence. The reference to the Intellect shining into the Will expresses Llull's conviction that rational argument can lead the soul to belief.
86 That is, all the Lover's internal and external senses are devoted to contemplating the Beloved.

127. ¶ A enteniment volentat ladrats e despertats los grans cans qui dormen ublidants mon amat A ulls plorats a cor suspirats a memoria membrats la desonor de mon amat la qual li fan aquells que ell ha tan honrats

Ha intellectus et voluntas latrate. evigilent per vos magni canes qui dormiunt obliviscentes amati mei? ullulate omnes aves celi. ha memoria mea recordare improperii et vituperiorum amati mei illatorum ab his quos honore maximo extulit.

128. ¶ Muntiplica la enamistat qui es enfre les gents e [212r] mon amat e promet dons e guardons mon amat e menaça ab justicia saviea e memoria e volentat menyspreen ses menaçes e sos prometimens

Multiplicata est inimicicia gentium adversus amatum meum. qui promitit mercedem et munera. minaturque per iusticiam et sapientiam. memoria autem et voluntas spernunt minas eius et promissiones.

129. ¶ Acostavas lamat al amich per ço quel aconsolas el conortas dels languiments que sostenia e dels plors que havia e on mes lamat a lamich sacostava pus fortment plorava e languia lamich per les desonors que planyia de son amat

Adherebat amato amicus ut ab eo consolaretur in langoribus et fletibus quos ferebat. quanto autem plus adherebat amato amicus tanto plus flebat et languebat. propter dedecus amati sui super quod plangebat

130. ¶ Ab ploma damor e ab aygua de plors e en carta de passio scrivia lamich unes letres a son amat en les quals li dehia que devocio se tardava e amor se muria e falliment e error muntiplicaven sos enemichs

Amoris scalamo et fletuum aqua in carta passionis scripsit amato suo [amicus *in margin*] epistolam dicens. devotio tardat nimis. amor moritur. fraus et errores multiplicant inimicos [191ra] tuos.

131. ¶ Nuavençe les amors del amich e lamat ab membrança enteniment volentat per ço quel amich el amat nos partissen e la corda en que les dues amors se nuaven era de pensaments languiments suspirs e plors

Amores amici et amati se connectebant cum memoria intellectu et voluntate. ut alter ab altero non divideretur. funis autem per quem duo amores eorum connexi sunt ex cogitationibus. langoribus suspiriis et fletibus.

132. ¶ Jahia lamich en lit damor los lançols eren de plaers e lo cobertor era de languiments el cuxi era de plors e era questio sil drap del cuxi era del drap dels lançols o del cobertor

Iacebat amicus in lecto amoris cuius linteamina erant de placitis. coopertorium de langoribus et pulvinar de fletibus. Queritur utrum pannus pulvinaris esset de panno linteaminum vel coopertorii.

127. "O Intellect and Will, bark! Wake up the great sleeping hounds[87] that have forgotten my Beloved! O eyes, weep! O heart, sigh! O Memory, remember the dishonor done to my Beloved by those He has honored so much."

128. The animosity between people and my Beloved grows. Still, my Beloved promises gifts and rewards, and threatens with justice and wisdom. But Memory and Will scorn His threats and His promises.

129. The Beloved approached the Lover, in order to console and comfort him for the anguish he endured and the tears he shed. But the closer the Beloved came to the Lover, the more the Lover lamented, languished, and wept about the dishonor to his Beloved.

130. With a pen of love, ink of tears, and paper of passion the Lover wrote some letters to his Beloved. He said: "Devotion is overdue. Love is dying. Fraud and error increase your enemies."

131. The love between the Lover and the Beloved bound itself up with Memory, Intellect, and Will, so that the Lover and the Beloved would not separate. The cord that bound their love was made of anguish, longing sighs, and weeping.

132. The Lover lay in the bed[88] of love: the sheets were made of pleasure, the bedcover of anguish, and the pillow of weeping. So the question arose whether the cloth of the pillow came from the sheets or the cover.

---

87 Often interpreted in medieval exegesis to mean any prelates or preachers, the dogs here may refer specifically to the Dominicans, known in Latin by the punning nickname *domini canes* ("dogs of the Lord"). Llull often criticizes the mendicant orders' lack of attention to their missionary duties.
88 An image often interpreted in medieval exegesis as symbolic of conscience or contemplation.

133. ¶ Vestia lamat son amich mantell cota gonella e capell li fahia damor e camisa de pensaments e calçes de tribulacions e garlanda de plors

Induebat amatus amicum suum clamide. tunica et pileo amoris et camisia cogitationum. calciavit eum caligis tribulationum. sertum de fletibus inserebat capiti eius.

134. ¶ Pregava lamat son amich que no lublidas dehia lamich que nol pudia oblidar pus que nol pudia innorar

Rogabat amatus amicum dicens amice mi noli oblivisci mei. Inquit amicus ei. tui oblivisci nequeo cum te ignorare nequeam.

135. dehia lamat que en aquells lochs on es mes temut a loar lo loas el escusas dehia lamich que damor lo bastas Responia lamat [212v] que per samor sera encarnat e penjat per murir

ait illi amatus ubi plus laudari timeor in illis locis lauda et excusa me. dixit amicus ergo da mihi amoris sufficientiam. respondit amatus dicens illi. nonne pro te incarnatus sum? pro te intravi patibulum mortis?

136. ¶ Dehia lamich al seu car amat que li mostras manera con lo pogues fer conexer e amar e loar a les gents umpli lamat son amich de devocio pasciencia caritat tribulacions pensaments suspirs e plors e en lo cor del amich fo audacia en loar son amat e en sa bocá foren laors de son amat e en sa volentat fo menyspreament de lo blasme de les gents qui jutjan falsament

Inquit amicus amate. mi karissime ostende mihi modum et sapientiam ut possim te facere cognosci. amari et laudari ab hominibus. replevit amatus amicum suum. devotione paciencia. karitate. tribulationibus cogitationibus suspiriis et fletibus. surrexit in cor amici audacia ad laudandum amatum suum. In ore eius habundabant laudes amati sui. voluntas eius sprevit derisiones gentium false iudicantium.

137. ¶ Dehia lamich a les gents aquestes paraules Qui vertaderament remembra mon amat ublida en les circumstancies de son remembrament totes coses E qui totes coses oblida per membrar son amat de totes coses lo defen mon amat e part li dona de totes coses

Dixit amicus gentibus hos sermones. Qui vere amati [mei *in margin*] non reminiscitur. obliviscitur in circumstantibus recordationis sue omnia Et qui omnia obliviscitur ut amati mei recordetur? ab omnibus protegit eum amatus meus prestans ei de peccatis omnibus veniam.

133. The Beloved dressed His Lover: He made him a cape, coat, tunic, and helmet of love, a shirt of cares, shoes of suffering, and a garland of tears.[89]

134. The Beloved begged His Lover: "Lover, do not forget me." The Lover replied: "I cannot forget you, because I cannot ignore you."[90]

135. The Beloved told him to praise and defend Him in those places where it is hardest to speak His praise. The Lover said: "Give me enough love." The Beloved answered: "Did I not become flesh for you? Was I not put to death for you?"

136. The Lover asked his dear Beloved to show him a way that he could make people know, love, and praise Him. The Beloved filled the Lover with devotion, patience, love, tribulation, cares, longing sighs, and weeping. Then the heart of the Lover dared to acclaim his Beloved, his mouth was filled with praise for his Beloved, and his Will scorned the criticism of people who judge falsely.[91]

137. The Lover spoke these words to people: "Those who truly remember my Beloved forget everything around them when remembering. Those who forget everything else in order to remember my Beloved, my Beloved defends them from everything and forgives them from every sin."

138. They asked the Lover where love was born, how it lived, and how it died. The Lover answered that love was born from remembering, lived from understanding, and died from being forgotten.

---

89 The penitential character of this garb offers an illustrative contrast with the more militant character of Saint Paul's well-known "armor of God" (Ephesians 6.13-16).

90 Another example of the necessary mutual operation of the Memory and Intellect or Will.

91 A vague allusion, perhaps referring to Llull's own critics or even to unbelievers in general (because they do not correctly recognize or "judge" Christian truth).

138. ¶ Demanaren al amich de que nexia amor ni de que vivia ni per que muria Respos lamich que amors nexia del remembrament e vivia de intelligencia e muria per ublidament

Interrogaverunt quidam amicum dicentes. Unde nascitur amor? de quo vivit quare moritur? respondit amicus amor nascitur de recordationibus. vivit de intelligentia. moritur oblivione.

139. ¶ Hublida lamich tot ço qui es dejus lo subira çel per ço quel enteniment pugues pus alt puyar a conexer lamat lo qual la volentat desiga preycar contemplar

Oblitus est amicus omnia que sub [summo *in margin*] celo sunt ut intellectus altius posset ascendere ad cognoscendum amatum quem voluntas predicare desiderat et contemplari.

140. ¶ Anavas lamich combatre per honrar son amat e mena en sa companyia fe sperança caritat justicia prudençia fortitudo temprança ab que vençes los enemichs de son amat fora vençut lamich si no li ajudas son amat a significar ses nobilitats a son amich

Intrabat amicus prelium ad honorandum amatum suum. duxitque secum in acie. fidem spem karitatem. iusticiam prudentiam fortitudinem et temperantiam cum quibus super inimicos amati sui triumpharet. Iam inceperat amicus succumbere. surrexit amatus in adiutorium ei ad significandum nobilitates suas.

141. ¶ passar volia lamich a la derrerana fi per la qual amava son amat e les altres fins donaven li embargament en son passatge e per aço lonchs desigs he [213r] pensaments daven al amich tristicia e languiment

Transire voluit amicus ad ultimum finem per quem amatum suum diligebat. Alii vero fines transitui eius ministrabant impedimentum. Ideo longa desideria et cogitationes amico conferebant tristiciam et langores.

142. ¶ gabavas e alegravas lamich en les noblees de son amat languia lamich per sobre cogitacions e pensaments e era questio qual sentia pus fortment ols plaers ols turments

Iactabat et letabatur amicus in nobilitatibus amati sui. languebat amicus propter superhabundantiam cogitationum Queritur que plus sentiebat aut placita aut tormenta

143. ¶ Misatge era lamich als princeps crestians e als infeels per son amat per ço quels mostras la art els començaments a conexer amar lamat

Nuncius erat amicus principibus christianis et infidelibus pro amato suo ut ostenderet eis artem et principia ad cognoscendum et diligendum amatum.

139. The Lover forgot everything below the highest heaven, so that his Intellect could rise even higher to know the Beloved, whom the Will longs to preach and contemplate.

140. The Lover went out to fight for the honor of his Beloved.[92] In his troops he led faith, hope, love, justice, prudence, fortitude, and temperance to vanquish the enemies of his Beloved. But the Lover would be defeated if his Beloved did not help him and thus display His excellence.

141. The Lover wished to reach the final goal in loving his Beloved, but other goals blocked his way. So great longing and care caused the Lover to feel anguish and sadness.[93]

142. The Lover gloried and rejoiced in the excellence of his Beloved. The Lover languished from so many cares and concerns. So the question arose: which did he feel most keenly, the pleasures or the torments?

143. The Beloved sent the Lover as a messenger to Christian princes and to unbelievers, in order to show them the method and principles[94] of knowing and loving the Beloved.

---

92 This common-place image of the "Army of the Seven Virtues" usually opposes the "Host of Seven Sins". By enlisting these troops to fight for the honor of the Beloved, this scene implies a penitential lesson: Christians must exercise virtue in order to avoid dishonoring God.

93 Perhaps an allusion to Llull's doctrine of the "first and second intentions" (ultimate and intermediary purposes) that define every creature's relation to the Creator.

94 Presumably the method and principles of Llull's Great Art. Llull sought support for his work from king James II of Aragon and king Philip of France, as well as from several popes and various academic authorities, but with little success.

144. ¶ Si veus amador honrat de nobles vestimens honrat per vanagloria gras per menjar e durmir Sapies que en aquell veus dampnacio e turments E si veus amador pobrement vestit menyspreat per les gents descolorit e magre per dejunar e vetlar Sapies que en aquell veus salvacio e perdurable benediccio

Dixit amatus ad amicum. si videas amatorem nobilibus vestimentis decoratum inani gloria veneratum. epulis fertilibus et diuturno sompno quieto impingatum scias dampnationem vides in eum et tormenta. Si autem vi[191rb]deas amatorem habitu paupertatis indutum a gentibus spretum et vituperatum. ieiunio et vigiliis maceratum. tu quidem vides in eo salvationem et benedictionem.

145. ¶ plany se lamich e clamas lo cor de calor damor mor se lamich ploral lamat e dona li consolacio de paciencia sperança guaardo

Plangebat amicus. cor eius conquerabatur de amore. moriebatur amicus. plorabat amatus super eum dans ei consolationem. pacientiam. spem et mercedem.

146. ¶ plorava lamich ço que havia perdut e no era quil pugues consolar per ço cor sos perdiments eren inrecuperables

Plorabat amicus pro hiis que perdiderat. nec erat qui consolari posset eum quia eius perdita irrecuperalia erant.

147. ¶ Creada ha deus la nit a cogitar e a vetlar lamich en les [noblees *in margin*] de son amat e cuydavas lamich que la hagues creada a reposar e a dormir aquells qui son treballats per amor

Deus creavit noctem ad cogitandum et vigilandum in nobilitatibus amati. opinabatur autem amicus quod deus creasset eam . ad requiescendum et dormiendum eis qui ab amore fatigati sunt.

148. ¶ Escarnien e reprenien les gents lamich per ço cor anava com a foll per amor El amich menyspreava lurs scarns e reprenia les gents per ço cor no amaven son amat

Irridebat amicum turba gentium arguentes eum. eo quod ibat tanquam fatuus propter amorem amicus autem spernebat derisiones hominum eos redarguens eo quod non diligebant amatum suum.

149. ¶ Dehia lamich vestit son de drap vilment mas amor vest de plaents pensaments mon cor e lo cors de plors languiments passions

Dixit amicus paupertatis amictu vestitus sum. Amor autem cor meum induit decoris cogitationibus et corpus meum fletibus langoribus et passionibus.

144. The Beloved said to the Lover: "If you see a Lover distinguished by noble clothes, honored with vain pride, and fat from overeating and untroubled sleep, you surely see damnation and torment in him. But if you see a Lover poorly clothed, scorned by people, pale and weak from fasting and vigils, you surely see salvation and eternal blessing in him."[95]

145. The Lover weeps and his heart calls out in the heat of love. The Lover dies. The Beloved weeps for him, and gives him the consolation of patience, hope, and reward.

146. The Lover wept over what he had lost and no one could console him, because what he lost was irreplaceable.[96]

147. God created the night for the Lover to meditate on the excellence of his Beloved in vigils. But the Lover thought He created it so those exhausted from travails of love could rest and sleep.[97]

148. A crowd of people mocked and scolded the Lover because he went around like a fool for love. But the Lover scorned their mockery and scolded the people because they did not love his Beloved.

149. The Lover said: "I wear wretched rags, but love clothes my heart with attractive cares, and my body with tears, anguish, and suffering."

---

95 An excellent example of how Llull extends the interpretative functions of spiritual "seeing" into a generalized exercise of moral allegory, so that all human behavior offers an ethical lesson.

96 Perhaps an allusion to Paradise or to the salvation of unbelievers.

97 Paragraphs 147 through 149 offer implicit contrasts between the welfare of the soul and of the body.

150. ¶ Can[213v]tava lamat e dehia endreçen se los meus loadors en loar mes valors e los enemichs de mos honraments turmenten los e han los en menyspreament E per aço he trames a mon amich que planga e plor ma desonor els seus plants els seus plors son nats de mes amors

Cantabat amatus dicens. ego direxi laudantes me ad laudandum valores meos. Inimici autem decorum meorum persecuntur et cruciantur eos despicientes eos. ideo misi amico meo ut plangat cum fletu et lacrimis propter obprobrium et dedecus illatum mihi. planctus eius et fletus cum lacrimis orti sunt de amoribus meis.

151. ¶ Jurava lamich al amat que per samor amava e sostenia treballs e passions e per aço pregava lamat quel amas e de sos trebaylls passio hagues Jura[va *deleted*] lamat que natura e proprietat [de saviea *deleted*] era de samor que amas tots aquells quil amaven e que hagues pietat daquells qui per samor treball sostenien Alegras lamich e consolas en la natura e en la proprietat essencial[s *deleted*] de son amat

Iurabat amicus amato propter eius amorem se sustinuisse labores et passiones. hortabatur ideo amatum ut laborum suorum et passionum reminisceretur. Iurabat amatus naturam et proprietatem amoris sui esse eum diligere omnes diligentes se et misereri omnibus qui propter amorem eius tribulationem paciuntur letabatur amicus et consolatus est in essentiali natura et proprietate amati sui.

152. ¶ Veda la paraula lamat a son hamich e aconsolavas lamich lamich en lesguardament de son amat

Verba prohibuit amatus amico suo. consolabatur amicus in conspectu sui ad amatum.

153. ¶ Tant plora e crida lamich a son amat tro quel amat devalla de les altees subiranes dels cels e vench en terra plorar e planyer e murir per amor e per nudrir los homens a amar e a conexer loar sos honraments

Tam diu ploravit amicus clamando amatum suum. usquequo a summa celorum altitudine descendit amatus in terram ad plorandum et plangendum et moriendum propter amorem ut enutriret homines ad cognoscendum ad amandum et ad laudandum honores eius.

154. ¶ blasmava lamich los crestians com no meten lo nom de son amat jhesu crist primerament en lurs letres per ço que li faesen la honor quels sserrayns fan a mafumet qui fo home galiador al qual fan honor con lo nomenen primerament en lurs letres

Arguebat amicus christianos pro eo quod nomen amati sui ihesu christi in epistolis suis non prescribebant. cum nobilius et dignius magisque honorificum sit nomen christi qui deus est et homo preponi a christianis quam nomen machometi a sarracenis qui nomen eius suis scriptis premitere consueverunt qui fuit pseudoprophetarum et anima eius dolo et malitia habundavit

150. The Beloved was singing and said: "Those who praise me become righteous by praising my worthiness, even though the enemies of my honor torment and scorn them. So I have ordered my Lover to lament and mourn my dishonor. His tears and weeping are born from my love."

151. The Lover swore to the Beloved that for His love he loved to endure travail and suffering. So he begged the Beloved to love him and to have compassion on his travail. The Beloved swore that it was the natural property of His love to love all those who loved Him and to have mercy on those who bore travails for His love. The Lover rejoiced and took comfort in the essential property of his Beloved.[98]

152. The Beloved ordered His Lover not to speak. So the Lover consoled himself watching his Beloved.

153. The Lover wept and called for his Beloved until He descended from the heights of the highest heavens. He came to earth to weep, lament, and die for love, and to train people to love, know, and praise His excellence.

154. The Lover criticized Christians for not putting the name of his Beloved Jesus Christ first in their correspondence. They should do Him the honor that the Muslims do to the evil rogue and false prophet Mohammed when they honor him by naming him first in their correspondence.

---

98   Scholastic logic and metaphysics treat property as a defining characteristic of a species, but distinct from a species's essence. Llull often less rigorously identifies properties as essential characteristics.

155. ¶ encontra lamich un scuder qui anava consiros he era magre descolorit e pobrement vestit e saluda lamich dient que deus lendreças a trobar son [214r] amat el amich li demana en que lavia conegut el escuder li dix que los uns secrets damors revelen los altres E per aço han conexença los amadors los uns dels altres

Obviavit amicus uni scutifero incedenti consideroso macerato et decolorato pannoque paupertatis induto. qui salutavit amicum dicens. dirigat te deus ad inveniendum amatum tuum. mirabatur amicus dicens. in quo cognovisti me. scutifer ait illi, secreta amorum alia revelant alia ob hoc habent amatores alii aliorum cognitionem

156. ¶ les noblees els honraments e les bones obres del amat son tresor e riquees del amich e lo tresor del amat son los pensaments els desigs els turments els plors els languiments quel amich soste per honrar e amar son amat

Nobilitates et honores atque bona opera amati sunt thesaurus et divicie amici. thesaurus autem amati sunt cogitationes desideria tormenta fletus et langores que amicus sustinet ad honorandum amatum suum.

157. ¶ Grans osts e grans companyes se son ajustades de spirits damors e porten senya damor on es la figura el senyal de lur amat e no volen menar en lur companyia null home qui sia sens amor per ço que lur amat no y prenga desonor

Exercitus maximus congregatus erat amoris spirituum portantium amoris vexillum in figura et signo amati sui. nolunt in acie sua ducere quemquam qui amore exutus sit ne amato suo dedecus inde contingat.

158. ¶ los homens quis depenyen folls per ajustar diners moven lamich a esser foll per amor e la vergonya quel amich ha de les gents a anar com a foll dona manera al amich don haja amor e preu de les gents E per aço es questio qual dels dos moviments es major occasio damor

Homines pro [191va] pecunia se fingentes fatuos. amicum monent esse fatuum pro amore. pudor autem quem amicus a gentibus patitur eundo tamquam fatuus . prestat illi modum quomodo precium et amorem a gentibus optineat Queritur quis duorum motuum maior est amoris occasio.

159. ¶ En tristicia ha amor mes lamich per sobre cogitaments e canta lamat he alegras lamich com lach oit e fo questio qual dels .ii. fo major occasio a muntiplicar amor en lamich

In tristiciam iecit amicum amor propter superhabundantiam cogitationum. cantavit amatus. letabatur amicus audito amato. Queritur quis duorum maior causa fuit multiplicationis amoris in amicum.

155. The Lover met a squire who was walking along lost in thought, weak, pale, and poorly dressed.[99] He greeted the Lover and said: "May God lead you to find your Beloved." The Lover was amazed and asked: "How did you recognize me?" The squire replied: "The secrets of love reveal one another. In this way Lovers recognize one another."

156. The dignity, excellence, and good works of the Beloved are the treasure and riches of the Lover. The treasure of the Beloved are the cares, desires, torments, weeping, and anguish that the Lover endures in order to honor and love his Beloved.

157. Great troops and brigades assemble in the spirit of love. They bear the flag of love with the image and sign of their Beloved. They refuse to take in their company anyone lacking love, in order to avoid dishonoring their Beloved.

158. People who foolishly heap up money compel the Lover to be a fool for love. The shame that people feel when the Lover goes around like a fool offers the Lover a way to earn love and respect from people. So the question arises, which of the two reactions is a greater cause of love?[100]

159. Love made the Lover sad from too much meditating. So the Beloved sang and the Lover became happy when he heard it.[101] So the question arises, which of these two occasions most increased love in the Lover?

---

99 The kind of chance encounter often depicted in romances and other chivalric literature. The squire's appearance clearly suggests that he is another Lover.

100 Here the Lover's "foolishness" clearly serves traditional Christian ideals of poverty and teaching by example, unlike the sufi "foolishness" that strives to promote separation from mundane affairs.

101 Perhaps the "voice of the Beloved" (Song of Songs 2.8 or 5.2).

160. ¶ En los secrets del amich son revelats los secrets del amat e en los secrets del amat son revelats los secrets del amich e es questio qual dels .ii. secrets es major occasio de revelacio

In secretis amici revelantur amati secreta. In secretis autem amati revelantur amici secreta. Queritur quid duorum secretorum maior est revelationis ocasio.

161. ¶ demanaren al foll per quals senyals [214v] era conegut son amat Respos e dix que per misericordia pietat estant en volentat essencialment sens negu camiament

Dic amice fatue quo signo cognoscitur amatus tuus. respondit amicus per misericordiam et pietatem in voluntate existens essentialiter absque alteratione.

162. ¶ Per la special amor quel amich havia al amat amava lo be comu sobre lo be special per ço que comunament fos son amat conegut loat desirat

Propter specialem amorem quem amicus ad amatum habuit dilexit amicus commune bonum super speciale bonum ut communiter amatus suus cognosceretur diligeretur laudaretur et desideraretur.

163. ¶ Amor e desamor sencontraren en un verger on parlaven secretament lamich el amat e amor demana a desamor per qual entencio era venguda en aquel loch e respos desamor que per desenamorar lamich e per desonrar lamat molt desplach al amat e al amich ço que dehia desamor e muntiplicaren amor per ço que vençes e destruis desamor

Obviaverunt sibi amor et odium in viridario ubi secrete loquebantur amatus et amicus. interrogavit amor odium qua intentione venisti in hunc locum. respondit. ut essem in amico ad vituperandum amatum. Multum displicuerunt amato et amico sermones odii et amorem multiplicaverunt ut devinceret et destrueret odium.

164. ¶ Digues foll en quet sens major volentat o en amar o en airar Respos que en amar per ço cor ayrava per tal que pogues amar

Dic fatue in quo intelligitur maior voluntas? aut in diligere vel in odire? qui respondit in diligere quia odiebat ut posset diligere.

165. ¶ Digues amador en que has mes de enteniment o en entendre veritat o falsetat Respos que en entendre veritat per que cor enten falsetat per ço que puscha mills entendre veritat

Dic amator ubi est plus intellectus aut in intelligere veritatem aut falsitatem Qui respondit. in intelligere veritatem. quia falsitas intelligenda est ut veritas intelligatur.

160. The secrets of the Lover reveal the secrets of the Beloved and the secrets of the Beloved reveal the secrets of the Lover. So the question arises, which of the two secrets is the greater occasion for revelation?

161. They asked the fool: "What signs make your Beloved known?" He answered: "Mercy and pity, existing essentially and unchanging in the Will."[102]

162. Thanks to the individual love that the Lover had for the Beloved, he loved the general good above the individual good. In this way his Beloved would be generally loved, known, praised, and desired.[103]

163. Love and hate met in a garden where the Lover and Beloved spoke secretly. Love asked hate: "Why did you come to this place?" Hate said: "To make the Lover ignore and dishonor the Beloved." What hate said displeased the Beloved and the Lover very much: they increased love so it would conquer and destroy hate.

164. "Say, fool! Do you feel your Will more when loving or when hating?" He replied when loving, because he hated in order to be able to love.

165. "Say, Lover! Does your Intellect comprehend more when understanding truth or falsehood?" He replied when understanding truth. "Why?" "Because I understand falsehood in order to understand truth better."[104]

---

102 Presumably in God's Will, but continually manifested in divine grace and justice toward humans.

103 Where paragraph 161 identifies the relationship between the one Beloved and His many Lovers, this paragraph defines the relationship of the individual Lovers to their common Beloved.

104 Llull often recommends this kind of cognition through contraries, perhaps in imitation of contemporary moral literature, which routinely urges sinners to know each vice by recognizing its opposing virtue.

166. ¶ Apercebe lamich que era amat per son amat e demana al amat si sa amor e sa misericordia eren en ell una cosa matexa Atorga lamat que en sa essencia no han diferencia sa amor ni sa misericordia E per aço dix lamich per quel turmentava sa amor e per que nol guaria sa misericordia de ses languors e repos lamat que la misericordia li dona les langors per ço que ab aquelles honras pus perfetament sa amor

Percepit amicus se diligi ab amato. quesivit ab amato utrum eius amor et misericordia essent idem in eo. concessit amatus in essentia sua nullam esse differentiam inter eius misericordiam et amorem. tunc ait amicus illi quare ergo misericordia tua non sanat me a langoribus meis. respondit amatus ei misericordia tibi langores tribuit ut per eos vehementius amorem honores

167. ¶ lamich volch anar en una terra stranya per honrar son a[215r]mat e volch se desmerxar per ço que no fos pres en lo cami e tant no poch desmerxar de sos hulls plors ni de sa cara magres fayçons e groga color ni de son cor plants pensaments suspirs tristicia languiments E per aço fo pres en lo viatge e liurat aturments per los enemics de son amat

In terram alienam voluit amicus proficisci ad honorandum amatum suum Voluit se dissimulari ne caperetur in via. dissimulari autem non potuit fletus ab oculis suis nec maciem nec colorem croceum a facie sua. nec planctus. cogitationes suspiria. tristiciam et langores a corde suo. Ideo captus est in itinere et suppliciis traditus ab inimicis amati sui.

168. ¶ Estava pres lamich en lo carçre damor pensaments desigs e remembraments lo guardaven ol encadenaven per ço que no fugis a son amat languiments lo turmentaven paciencia sperança lo consolaven moriras lamich mas- lamat li demonstra son estament e reviscola lamich

Captus erat amicus in amoris carcere. custodes eius erant cogitationes recordationes et desideria que ut non ab amato suo fugeret concatenabant eum. langores cruciabantur eum. spes autem et pacientia eum consolabantur. moreretur amicus sed amatus statum suum insinuavit ei et vivificatus est.

169. ¶ Encontra lamich son amat conech lamich son amat e plora repres lamat son amich per ço cor no plorava ans que la agues conegut e demana li en que lavia conegut pus que no plorava Respos lamich que en lo remembrament e en lenteniment e en sa volentat on fo multiplicament encontinent que fo present a sos ulls corporals

Obviavit amicus amato suo. cognovit amatum amicus et lacrimatus est. reprehendit amatus amicum dicens. quare non lacrimatus es priusquam me cognosceres. in quo ergo cognovisti me priusquam non lacrimaberis? respondit amicus in rememoratione et intellectu. confestim dum presens affuisti corporalibus oculis meis.

166. The Lover perceived that he was loved by his Beloved. He asked the Beloved if His love and mercy were one single thing in Him. The Beloved confessed that in His essence there is no difference between love and mercy. So the Lover asked: "Why does your love torment me and your mercy not cure me of my anguish?" The Beloved said to him: "Mercy caused your anguish, so that you would honor love more fully with it."[105]

167. The Lover decided to visit a strange land in order to honor his Beloved. He decided to disguise himself to avoid being captured on the way. But he could not disguise the tears in his eyes, the weak appearance and yellow color of his face, or the laments, cares, sighs, sadness, and anguish in his heart. So he was captured on the journey and turned over to the enemies of his Beloved to be tortured.[106]

168. The Beloved sat captive in the prison of love. Cares, desires, and memories guarded him in chains so he could not escape to his Beloved. Anguish tormented him. Patience and hope consoled him. The Lover would have died, but the Beloved revealed His own condition to the Lover and revived him.[107]

169. The Lover met his Beloved, recognized his Beloved, and wept. The Beloved scolded His Lover and said: "Why were you not weeping before you recognized me? How did you recognize me when you were not weeping?" The Lover answered: "Through Memory, Intellect, and Will, which increased as soon as you appeared to my eyes."[108]

---

105 A solution to the problem of distinguishing separate attributes in the Godhead, which is critical to Llull's own doctrine of Divine Dignities. Here he suggests that God is absolutely unitary, but causes diverse effects among creatures.

106 Perhaps another allusion to Llull's own imprisonment while preaching in North Africa; see the note on paragraph 52.

107 The spiritual prison of love for the Beloved contrasts with the material prison of the Lover's tormentors in paragraph 167.

108 Throughout his oeuvre, Llull insists that information gathered from the Senses may stimulate the mind, but is never sufficient in itself for attaining spiritual knowledge, which requires the operation of the higher faculties of the soul.

170. ¶ Demana lamat al amich que era amor Respos que presencia de fayçons e de
paraules damat en cor suspirant damador e languiment per desig e per plors en cor
damich

Interrogavit amatus amicum dicens. quid est amor? respondit amicus presentia
speciose faciei amati et eius collocutiones in amatoris corde [191vb] suspirante. et
langores per fletus et per desideria in corde amici.

171. ¶ Amor es bulliment daudacia e de temor per frevor e amor es final volentat a
desirar son amat e amor [es *in margin for deleted* d] aquella cosa qui auçis lamich
con ohi cantar de les bellees de son amat e amor es ço en que es ma mort e en que
esta tots jorns ma volentat
amor est ebullitio audacie et timoris per fervorem. amor est finalis voluntas diligendi
amatum. amor est id quod occidit amicum dum audivit cantus pulcritudinis amati
sui. amor est id in quo mea mors est. et id in quo voluntas mea permanet semper.

172. ¶ Devocio e enyorament trameteren per misacgers pensaments al cor de lamich
per ço que pujas laygua als hulls qui volien [215v] cessar dels plors en los quals
havien longament estats

Devotio et contrictio per nuncios miserunt cogitationes in cor amici. ut ascenderet
aqua ad occulos volentes cessare a fletibus in quibus diu conversa [verant *corrected
from* varant]

173. ¶ dehia lamich si vosaltres amadors volets foch venits a mon cor e encenets
vostres lantees e si volets aygua venits als meus hulls qui decorren de lagremes E si
volets pensaments damor venits los pendre a mes cogitacions

Dicebat amicus. o vos amatores qui vultis ignem. venite ad cor meum incendite
lampades vestras. venite volentes aquam aurite ab oculis meis fluentibus lacrimis et
qui cogitationes amoris desiderant veniant ad cogitationes meas et replebuntur eis.

174. ¶ esdevench se un dia quel amich cogitava en la gran amor que havia a son
amat e en los grans treballs e perills en que havia estat longament per samor e
considera que sos guaardons fossen grans dementre quel amich cogitava en esta
manera el remembra que pagat lavia son amat per ço cor lavia enamorat de ses
fayçons e cor per samor li avia donats languiments

Quadam die amicus meditabatur in vehementi amore sui ut amatum in ingentisque
laboribus et periculis que diu passus fuerat amore eius. consideravit enim magna sibi
futura premia. dum autem isto modo meditaretur recoluit amatum solvisse ei quia
amati pulcritudinem dilexerat et quia amatus ei dederat pro amore suo langores.

170. The Beloved asked the Lover what love was. He replied: "The presence of the lovely appearance and words of the Beloved in the longing heart of the Lover, or the anguish of desire and weeping in the heart of the Lover."

171. "Love is courage and fear boiling with fervor. Love is longing for the Beloved as the ultimate desire. Love is what killed the Lover when he heard a song about the beauty of his Beloved. Love is where my death is and where my Will rests forever."[109]

172. Devotion and longing sent cares as messengers to the heart of the Lover, to make his eyes pour out water, but they wished to cease their constant weeping.

173. The Lover said: "If you Lovers want fire, come light your torches from my heart. If you want water, come to my eyes running with tears. If you want the cares of love, come take them from my meditations."

174. One day the Lover was meditating on the great love that he felt for his Beloved and the great travail and danger that he had known so long for His love. And he imagined that his rewards would be great. While the Lover was thinking this way, he remembered that his Beloved had already paid him, when He made him love His beauty and gave him anguish for his love.[110]

---

109 The metaphorical identification of love and death becomes a shibboleth of courtly love literature, but this paragraph seems equally indebted to the Pauline image of "dying to the flesh" (Romans 8) or to the use of similar expressions by sufi writers, who describe a self-mortification or annihilation of consciousness when the soul escapes to a higher state.

110 A clear illustration of a doctrine implied in many other paragraphs: humans should serve God from love, not from the hope of reward or from fear of punishment.

1⁷5. ¶ Torcava lamich sa cara e sos hulls de plors que sostenia per amor per ço que no descobris los languiments que li donava son amat lo qual dix a son amich per que celava los senyals damor als altres amadors los quals li havia donats per ço quels enamoras de honrar ses valors

Tergebat amicus vultum et oculos suos a lacrimis que pro amore sustinuit ut langores quos amatus ei dederat non revelaret. Inquit amatus illi. quare celas amatoribus signa amoris que tibi dedi. ut eos philocaperes ad honorandum valores meos?

176. ¶ Digues home qui vas com a foll per amor tro a quant de temps seras serf e sotsmes a plorar e a sostenir treballs e languiments Respos tro al temps con mon amat del anima e del cors fara en mi departiment

Dic eya homo stultus incedens. quanto tempore servus eris subiugatus ad plorandum et ad portandum mirabile pondus laboris et langoris. qui respondit. tanto tempore usquequo amatus meus anime mee et corporis fecerit disgressionem.

177. ¶ Digues foll has diners Respos he amat has viles ni castells ni ciutats comdats ni dugats Respos he amors pensaments plors desirers treballs languiments qui son mellors que emperis ni regnats [216r]

Dic fatue habes pecuniam? respondit amicus. amatum habeo. habes villas. habes castra, habes civitates. habes ducatus. respondit amicus habeo amores cogitationes. fletus desideria. tribulationes et langores que omnibus regnis et imperiis multo sunt meliora.

178. ¶ Demanaren al amich en que conexia la sentencia de son amat Respos que en la egualtat de plaers e languiments a la qual son amat jutjava sos amadors

Interrogaverunt amicum quidam dicentes in quo cognoscis sententiam amati tui? respondit amicus in equalitate placitorum et langorum in qua amatus meus iudicat amatores suos.

179. ¶ Digues foll qui sab mes damor o aquell qui na plaer o aquell qui na treballs e languiments Respos e dix que la .i. sens laltre non pot haver conexença

Dic fatue quis plus amoris habet aut qui in amore sentit placita aut qui pro amore tribulationes patitur et langores. respondit amicus neuter eorum absque hoc quod habet utraque

180. ¶ Demanaren al amich per que no sescusava dels falliments e delos falsos crims que les gents lacusaven Respos que a scusar havia son amat que les gents blasmaven falsament e que home on pot caer engan e error no es quaix digne de nulla escusacio

Dic amice cur non te excusas a falsitate et falsis criminibus que adversus te testificantur? respondit amicus excusare habeo amatum meum quem false gentes increpant. homo enim eo quod in fraudem et errorem potest cadere nulla est quasi dignus excusatione

175. The Lover wiped from his face and eyes the tears he shed for love, in order not to reveal the anguish caused by his Beloved. The Beloved asked him: "Why do you hide signs of love from other Lovers, when I gave you these to make them love to honor my worthiness?"

176. "Say, you who go around like a fool for love! How long will you be a slave forced to weep, enduring travail and anguish?" He replied: "Until my Beloved makes my soul leave my body."

177. "Say, fool, do you have money?" He replied: "I have a Beloved." "Do you have towns, castles, cities, counties, or dukedoms?" He replied: "I have love, cares, weeping, desire, travail, and anguish, which are better than any empire or kingdom."

178. They asked the Lover how he recognized the judgement of his Beloved. He replied in the sentences of equal pleasure and pain that his Beloved pronounced upon His Lovers.

179. "Say, fool, who knows love better, the one who gets pleasure from it or the one who gets trouble and anguish from it?" The Lover answered: "There can be no knowledge of one without the other."[111]

180. They asked the Lover: "Why do you not defend yourself against the false accusations of sin and crime that people make against you?"[112] The Lover replied: "I must defend my Beloved, because people falsely criticize Him. Humans, who fall easily into error and deception, scarcely deserve any defense."

---

111 Paragraphs 178 and 179 offer especially clear statements of this dominant theme.

112 It is not clear how the terms "sin" and "crime" would apply to Llull's own activities, although any layperson who tried to preach or teach theology publicly was liable to investigation and prosecution by authorities, as happened to his French contemporary, Marguerite Porete.

181. ¶ Digues foll per que scuses amor com treballa e turmenta ton cors e ton cor
Respos per ço cor multiplica mos merits e ma benauyrança
Dic amice fatue quare amorem excusas dum cor et corpus tuum vexat et cruciatur?
respondit amicus quia merita et beatitudinem mihi multiplicat.

182. ¶ Complanyias lamich de son amat com tan greument lo fahia turmentar a amor
e scusavas lamat muntiplicant al amich treballs e perills pensaments e lagremes e
plors
Conquerebatur amicus de amato suo quia tam graviter faciebat eum ab amore
tormentari. excusabat et amatus muitiplicando ei labores pericula cogitationes et
lacrimas cum fletibus

183. ¶ Digues foll per que scuses los colpables respos per ço que no sia semblant als
acusants los innocents els colpables
Dic fatue quare excusas culpabiles? qui respondit. ne innocentes et culpabiles sint
[accusantibus *in margin*] accusationibus similes.

184. ¶ Levava lamat lenteniment a entendre ses altees per ço quel amich enclinas
son remembrament a membrar sos defalliments e la volentat los menyspreas e pujas
amar los acabaments del amat
Elevabat amatus intellectum ad intelligendum altitudines suas ut amicus memoriam
suam inclinaret ad recolendum culpas suas et voluntatem ad despiciendum delicta
sua et elevaretur ad diligendum perfectiones amati sui.

185. ¶ Cantava lamich de son amat e dehia que tant li portava bona volentat que
totes les coses que airava per samor li eren [216v] plaents e benananges majors que
les coses que amava sens la amor de son amat
Cantabat amicus de amato suo dicens [192ra] tam bonam gero dilecto meo
voluntatem quod omnia que mihi odiosa fuerant. nunc amore eius mihi valde
placentia sunt magisque felicia omnibus hiis que absque amore dilecci mei diligebam

186. ¶ Anava lamich per una gran ciutat e demanava si trobaria null home ab qui
pogues parlar a ssa guisa de son amat e mostraren li un home pobre qui plorava per
amor e cerchava companyo ab qui pogues parlar damor
Ibat amicus per quandam civitatem querens aliquem hominem cum quo de amato
[*corrected from* amico] suo loqui posset ad placitum. cui insinuatus est homo
quidam pauper flens propter amorem et querens socium cum quo de amore loqui
posset.

181. "Say, fool, why do you defend love when it troubles and torments your heart and body?" He replied: "Because it increases my merit and ultimate happiness."

182. The Lover complained that his Beloved made love torment him severely. The Beloved defended Himself by increasing the travails, dangers, cares, tears, and weeping of the Lover.

183. "Say, fool, why do you defend the guilty?" He replied: "In order not to resemble those who accuse the innocent along with the guilty."[113]

184. The Beloved raised the Intellect of the Lover to understand His heights. In this way the Lover would lower his Memory to remember his faults. And his Will would scorn his failings and rise to love the perfections of the Beloved.[114]

185. The Lover sang of his Beloved and said: "I bear so much good will toward Him that anything hateful to me pleases me, thanks to loving Him, and is now more pleasant to me than the things I loved without loving my Beloved."

186. The Lover went about a great city, trying to find someone who would gladly speak with him about his Beloved. So they showed him a poor man who was weeping from love and seeking a companion to talk about love.

---

113 As in paragraph 180, it is not clear here how this advice applies to Llull's own activities. However, it does extend the loving devotion fostered in these 366 paragraphs to the larger problem of reforming Christian society, which the *Book of Blanquerna* treats extensively.
114 Another example of Llull's favored contemplative method of "ascent and descent".

187. ¶ Estava lamich pensiu e enbarbesclat com pudien pendre començamens sos treballs de les noblees de son amat qui a en si mateix tanta de benauyrança

Stabat amicus cogitans et stupefactus quomodo a nobilitatibus amati sui in se habenti tantam beatitudinem possent labores sui exordium sumere

188. ¶ Estaven les cogitacions del amich enfre ublidança de sos turments e enfre membrança de sos plaers cor los plaers que ha damor li obliden la malanança e los turments que soste per amor li remembren la benanança que ha per amor

Stabant cogitationes amici inter oblivionem tormentorum suorum et inter recordationem placitorum suorum. quia propter amoris placita obliviscebatur adversitatem et propter tormenta que pro amore ferebat? recolebat beatitudinem quam habebat per amorem

189. ¶ demanaren al amich si era possible cosa que son amat lo desenamoras respos que no dementre que la memoria membras el enteniment entenes les nobleses de son amat

Interrogaverunt quidam amicum dicentes. estne possibile quod amatus tuus te desistat amare? qui respondit. nequaquam. dum memoria mea recolit et intellectus meus intelligit nobilitates amati mei

190. ¶ Digues foll de ques fa la major comparacio e semblança Respos damich e amat demanaren li per qual raho Respos que per amor qui estava enframdos

Dic amice fatue de quo fit maior comparatio in similitudine. qui respondit. de amato et amico. Quare hoc? respondit amicus propter amorem qui inter ambos existit.

191. ¶ demanaren al amat si havia hauda null temps pietat Respos que si no agues auda pietat no hagra enamorat lamich nil agra turmentat de suspirs e de plors e de treballs e de langors

Dic amate habuistine umquam pietatem? qui respondit. nisi ego pietatem habuissem non philocepissem amicum nec tormentarem eum suspiriis. fletibus. tribulationibus et langoribus.

192. ¶ En .i. gran boscatge era la[217r]mich qui anava cerchar son amat e atroba veritat e falsetat quis constrastaven de son amat cor veritat lo loava e falsetat lo blasmava E per aço lamich crida amor que ajudas a veritat

In quodo heremo maximo erat amicus et ibat querens amatum suum invenitque veritatem et falstitatem obstantes inter se ad invicem de amato suo. quia veritas laudabat eum. falsitas verō ipsum vituperabat. ideo clamavit amicus amorem dicens. o amor auxiliare veritati.

187. The Lover stood rapt in thought: how could his travails come from the excellence of his Beloved, who has so much bliss in Himself?[115]

188. The cares of the Lover shift between forgetting his torments and remembering his pleasures. This is because the pleasures of love make him forget his misery, but the torments of love make him remember the happiness that it gives.

189. They asked the Lover: "Is it possible for your Beloved to stop loving you?" He replied: "No, not as long as my Memory remembers and my Intellect understands the excellence of my Beloved."

190. "Say, fool, what makes the best comparison or likeness?" He replied: "The Lover and the Beloved." They asked him why. The Lover said because of the love between the two.[116]

191. They asked the Beloved: "Have you ever felt pity?" He answered: "If I had not felt pity, I would not have made the Lover love, or tormented him with sighs, weeping, travails, and anguish."

192. The Lover went looking for his Beloved in a vast wilderness.[117] He came across truth and falsehood arguing about his Beloved: truth was praising Him and falsehood was criticizing Him. So the Lover called to love: "O love, help truth!"

---

115 The implicit answer to this question is the theme of many other paragraphs, such as 83, 86, 90, 115, 166, 309, 315-17, and 320.
116 An outstanding expression of the doctrine that theocentric resemblances pervade all being, whether real, mental, or verbal. Llull's Great Art requires this universal resemblance in order to sustain its wide-ranging use of arguments from identity or difference.
117 Almost always glossed in medieval exegesis as a metaphor for the world and its delights, but also for unbelievers (especially the Jews).

193. ¶ Vench temptacio al amich per ço que li absentas son amat e que la memoria se despertas e recobras la presencia de son amat membrant aquell pus fortment que nol avia membrat per ço que lenteniment mes a ensus fos levat a entendre e la volentat a amar son amat

Venit temptatio ad amicum ut celaret ei amatum suum. et ut memoria excitaret et revelaret amati sui presentiam recolendo ipsum vehementius quam prius recoluerat ut intellectus altius ascenderet ad intelligendum et voluntas ad amandum amatum suum.

194. ¶ Ublida .j. dia lamich son amat e membra en altre dia quel avia ublidat e en aquel dia en lo qual lamich membrava que son amat hublidat avia fo lamich en tristicia e en dolor e en gloria e en benanança per ublidament e per membrança

Quadam die amicus oblitus fuit amatum suum. in altera vero die recoluit quod eum oblitus fuerat existens tunc in tristicia et dolore. et per desiderium in gloria et beatitudine.

195. ¶ Tant fortment desirava lamich laors e honraments de son amat que duptava quels membras E tan fortment ayrava les desonors de son amat que duptava que les ayras E per aço lamich stava enbarbesclat enfre amor e temor per son amat

Ita vehementer desideravit amicus laudes et honores amati sui. quod eas dubitavit recolere et ita vehementer odiebat vituperia amati sui. quod dubitabat utrum odiret ea. ideo amicus stabat stupefactus inter amorem et timorem propter amatum suum.

196. ¶ Muria lamich per plaer e viu per languiments els plaers els turments sajustaven e sunien en esser una cosa matexa en la volentat del amich E per aço lamich en un temps mateix muria e vivia

Moriebatur amicus per placita et vivebat per langores. placita autem et tormenta se coniungebant et vivebant ut idem essent in voluntate amici. ideo amicus eodem tempore moriebatur et vivebat

197. ¶ Ublidar e innorar volra lamich son amat una ora tan solament per ço que agues alcun repos a sos languiments Mas cor li fora passio lublidament e la innorancia hac paciencia e exalça [217v] son enteniment e sa memoria a contemplar son amat

Oblivisci et ignorare vellet amicus amatum una hora solum ut langoribus suis aliquam inferret [requiem corrected from requietem]. sed quia oblivisci et ignorare passionem ei ferrent habuit pacientiam in velle suo et exaltavit memoriam et intellectum suum ad contemplandum amatum suum.

193. The Lover felt tempted to leave his Beloved, so that Memory would awaken and reveal the presence of his Beloved. By remembering Him harder than he remembered Him before, the Intellect would rise higher to understand his Beloved and the Will to love his Beloved.[118]

194. One day the Lover forgot his Beloved. The next day he remembered that he had forgotten Him. On the day the Lover remembered forgetting his Beloved, he felt pain and sadness and glory and happiness, from forgetting and remembering.

195. The Lover desired praise and honor for his Beloved so strongly that he doubted if he would remember them. But he hated dishonor to his Beloved so much that he doubted if he would hate it. And this left the Lover confused between love and fear for his Beloved.

196. The Lover was dying from pleasure and living from anguish. Pleasures and torments joined and became the same thing in the Will of the Lover. Because of this the Lover was dying and living at the same time.

197. The Lover wanted to forget and ignore his Beloved for just one hour, in order to get some relief from his anguish. But forgetting and ignoring made him suffer, so his Will became patient, and he raised his Intellect and Memory to contemplate his Beloved.

---

118 Paragraphs 193 through 198 all concern the paradoxical mental dialectic through which the Lover strives to enhance his love, faith, understanding, and recollection of the Beloved by compelling them to struggle with hate, doubt, ignorance, and forgetfulness.

198. ¶ Tant amava lamich son amat que de tot ço que li dehia lo crehia e tant lo desirava entendre que tot ço que volia dir volia entendre per rahons necessaries E per aço la amor del amich estava enfre creença e intelligencia

Tantum diligebat amicus amatum suum quia omnia que dixit credidit. tantum desiderabat eum intelligere quod omnia que de eo audivit volebat intelligere necessariis rationibus. idcirco amor amici inter credentiam et intelligentiam existebat

199. ¶ Demanaren al amich qual cosa era pus luny de son coratge e ell respos que desamor e demanaren li per qual rao respos que per ço cor ço qui era pus prop a son coratge era amor qui es contrari de desamor

Dic amice quid est quod plus distat a corde tuo? qui respondit. odium. [192rb] et quare odium? respondit. quia id quod cordi meo propinquius est est amor qui contrarius est odio.

200. ¶ Digues foll has enveja Respos hoc totes les vegades que ublit la larguea e les riquees de mon amat

Dic fatue pateris invidiam? qui respondit. utique quotiens obliviscor largitatem amati mei.

201. digues amador has riquea Respos que hoc amor has pobrea hoc amor per que per ço cor no es amor major e cor no enamora molts amadors a honrar los honraments de mon amat

Dic amator habes divitias? qui respondit. utique. scilicet amorem. Et quare amorem? respondit. quia plures non philocapit amatores ad honorandum honores amati mei.

202. ¶ Digues amant hon es ton poder Respos en lo poder de mon amat ab que tesforçes contra tos enemichs ab les forçes de mon amat ab quet conortes ab los tresors eternals de mon amat

Dic amice ubi est potestas tua? qui respondit in potestate amati mei. in quo ergo fortificaris contra inimicos tuos. respondit in fortitudine amati mei cum quo ergo solaris. respondit cum eternalibus thesauris amati mei.

203. ¶ Digues foll qual hames mes o la misericordia de ton amat o la justicia de son amat Respos que tant li covenia amar e tembre justicia que nulla majoritat de voler no devia haver en sa volentat a amar nulla cosa sobre la justicia de son amat

Dic fatue quam plus diligis aut misericordiam aut iusticiam amati tui? qui respondit. tantum oportet me timere et diligere iusticiam quod nulla volendi maioritas esse debet in voluntate mea ad amandum quicquam super voluntatem amati mei.

198. The Lover loved his Beloved so much that he believed everything He said. But he longed to understand Him so much that he wanted proof[119] of everything he heard. So the love of the Lover stood between believing and understanding.

199. They asked the Lover: "What is furthest from your heart?" He answered: "Hate." They asked him why. He said: "Because the thing closest to my heart is love, which is the opposite of hate."

200. "Say, fool, are you envious?" He answered: "Yes, whenever I forget about the generosity and wealth of my Beloved."

201. "Say, Lover, are you rich?" He answered: "Yes, with love." "Are you poor?" "Yes, in love." "How?" "Because love is not greater and few Lovers are inspired to honor the excellence of my Beloved."

202. "Say, Lover, where does your power come from?" He answered: "From the power of my Beloved." "How do you resist your enemies?" "With the strength of my Beloved." "How do you comfort yourself?" "With the eternal treasures of my Beloved."[120]

203. "Say, fool, which do you love most: the mercy or the justice of your Beloved?" He answered: "It is so right for me to love and fear justice, that my Will should have no greater desire to love anything beyond the Will of my Beloved."

---

119 Literally, "necessary reasons", the kinds of arguments that Llull used in his Great Art and regarded as invincible.

120 That is, the expectation of enjoying God's eternal glory. However, paragraph 203 immediately adds that the best motive to serve God is love, rather than the hope of reward or fear of punishment.

204. ¶ Combatien se colpes e merits en la consciencia e en la volentat del amich e justicia membrança muntiplicaven consciencia e misericordia sperança muntiplicaven benanança [218r] en la volentat del amat e per aço los merits vencien colpes e torts en la penitencia del amich

Inter se preliabantur culpe et merita. in conscientia et voluntate amici. iusticia autem et recordatio conscientiam multiplicabant. misericordia vero et spes beatitudinem multiplicabant in voluntate amati. Ideo merita vincebant culpas et iniurias in amici penitentia.

205. ¶ Afermava lamich que en son amat era tota perfeccio e negava que en son amat no havia null defalliment e per aço era questio qual era major o la afermacio o la negacio

Affirmabat amicus in amato suo omnem invenire perfectionem negans in amato suo omne defectum. ideo queritur que istarum sit maior aut affirmatio aut negatio

206. ¶ Eclipse fo en lo cel e tenebres en la terra e per aço lamich remembra que peccat li havia longament absentat son amat de son voler per la qual absençia tenebres havien exilada la lugor de son enteniment ab la qual se representa lamat a sos amadors

Eclipsis fuit in celo et tenebre in terra. idcirco amicus recordatus est quod peccatum diu celaverat ei amatum suum a velle suo per cuius absentiam lux intellectus sui exulaverat a tenebris cum [qua in margin] se representat amatus amatoribus suis.

207. ¶ Vench amor en lamich a la qual amor lamich demana que volia e amor li dix que ella era venguda en ell per ço quel acustumas el nudris en tal manera que a la mort pogues vençre sos mortals enemichs

Venit amor in amicum [quem subst. in margin for cui] interrogavit amicus dicens quid vis mihi amor? cui respondit amor dicens. ego alumpne mi in te veni ut ita te nutriam ut possis vincere morti mortales inimicos tuos.

208. ¶ Malalta fo amor con lamich ublida son amat e malalte es lamich cor per sobre membrar son amat li dona treballs ansies e languiments

Infirmabatur amor dum amicus amatum obliviscebatur. amicus autem infirmabatur quia propter superhabundantiam recolendi amatum suum prestabat amatus ei tribulationes. langores et anxietates.

204. Sin and merit fought in the conscience and Will of the Lover. Then justice and Memory increased conscience while mercy and hope increased happiness in his Will. So merit defeated sin and injustice in the penitence of the Lover.[121]

205. The Lover affirmed that every perfection existed in his Beloved and denied that there was any imperfection in his Beloved. So the question arose: which was greater, the affirmation or the negation?

206. There was an eclipse in the sky and shadows fell on the earth. This made the Lover remember that sin had kept his Beloved from his Will for a long time. Because of His absence, darkness had driven from his Intellect the light with which the Beloved reveals Himself to His Lovers.[122]

207. Love visited the Lover. The Lover asked: "Love, what do you want with me?" Love told him: "I have come to train and raise you, my pupil, in such a way that when you die you can defeat your mortal enemies."[123]

208. Love became sick when the Lover forgot his Beloved. Now the Lover is sick, because his Beloved gave him travail, anxiety, and anguish through too much remembering.

---

121 Llull only mentions penitence three times in this text (here and in paragraphs 122 and 336-37), each time in connection with conscience or contrition. The repeated combination of these terms reveals the kind of fixed semantic associations that guide many of Llull's metaphorical and allegorical expressions.

122 This paragraph in effect interprets the metaphorical sense of the darkness imagery that it employs. See also the note on paragraphs 123-24.

123 That is, overcome the deadly sins and thus gain eternal life.

209. ¶ Atroba lamich un home que muria sens amor plora lamich la desonor quel
amat prenia en la mort daquel home qui muria sens amor e dix a aquell home per que
muria sens amor e ell respos que per ço cor no avia qui li hagues donada conexença
damor ni qui lagues nudrit a esser amador e per aço lamich suspira en plorant e dix a
devocio quant serets major per ço que la colpa sia menor e que lo meu amat aja molts
frevents ardits loadors amadors qui no dubten a loar sos honramens

Invenit amicus quendam hominem absque amore morientem. ploravit amicus
propter dedecus quod inferebatur amato in morte illius hominis absque amore
morientis. dixitque illi. homo quare moreris absque amore? ille vero respondit
dicens quia illo carui qui me cogitationem amoris docuisset. non habui qui me
nutriverit ad essendum amatorem. quo audito suspiravit amicus flendo dicens. ha
devotio quando eris maior ut culpa sit minor eo quod amatus meus multos ferventes
habeat et audaces amatores non dubitantes laudare honores eius?

210. ¶ Tempta lamich amor sis poria sostenir en son [218v] coratge sens que no
remembras son amat e cessa son cor de pensar e sos ulls de plorar e anichilas amor e
romas lamich enbarbesclat e demana a les gents si havien vista amor

Temptavit amicus amorem utrum posset se sustinere in corde suo. licet amatum
suum non recoleret. tunc cessavit cor amici a cogitationibus et oculi eius a fletibus
anichilatus est amor. amicus restitit stupefactus querens ab hominibus si vidissent
amorem.

211. ¶ Amor amar amich e amat se covenen tant fortment en lamat que .i. actualitat
son en essencia e diversses coses son lamich e lamat concordants sens nulla
contrarietat e diverssitat de essencia E per aço lamat es amable sobre totes altres
amors

Amor. amare. amicus et amatus tantam habent concordantiam quod in una
actualitate sunt in essentia. diverse vero res sunt amatus et amicus concordantes
absque aliqua contrarietate et diversitate essentie. ideo amatus amabilis est super
omnes alios amores.

212. ¶ digues foll per que has tan gran amor Respos cor lonch e perillos es lo viatge
en lo qual vaig cerchar mon amat ab gran feix lom cove encerchar e hivaçosament
me cove anar e totes aquestes coses no puria cumplir sens gran amor

Dic fatue cur tantum geris amorem? qui respondit quia longa et periculosa est
peregrinatio in qua pergunt homines querentes amatum meum. magno autem
pondere oportet me querere eum. velociter etiam oportet me ire. nec aliquod
[192va] istorum possem adimplere nisi amorem maximum gererem.

209. The Lover found a man who was dying without love.[124] The Lover wept at the dishonor done to his Beloved by the death of this man dying without love. So he asked the man: "Why are you dying without love?" He answered: "Because no one ever taught me to recognize love or trained me to be a Lover." Then the Lover groaned, wept, and cried: "Ah, devotion! When will you grow so that sin shrinks and my Beloved has many fervent, ardent, cheering Lovers who do not hesitate to praise His excellence?"

210. The Lover tested whether he could sustain love in his heart without remembering his Beloved. But his heart stopped worrying, his eyes stopped weeping, love vanished, and the Lover was left perplexed. He asked everybody if they had seen love.

211. Love, loving, the Lover, and the Beloved go together so strongly in the Beloved that they exist actively and essentially as one thing.[125] The Lover and Beloved remain different, but in concord together without any essential contrariety or diversity. Therefore the Beloved is lovable above all other loves.

212. "Say, fool, why is your love so great?" He answered: "Because the journey in search of my Beloved is long and dangerous. I must look for Him while carrying a heavy burden and I must go quickly. I could do none of this without great love."

---

124   Perhaps a personification of all unbelievers.
125   An example of Lullian "spiritual metaphysics", created from conventional Scholastic categories and terms for analyzing being.

213. ¶ Vetlava dejunava plorava almoyna fahia en terres stranyes anava lamich per ço que pugues a son amat moure sa volentat a a enamorar sos sotsmeses per honrar sos honraments

Vigilabat amicus. ieiunabat. plorabat. erogabat. per terras alienas ibat ut voluntatem amati sui commovere posset ad philocapiendum servos eius ut honorarent honores eius.

214. ¶ Si no abasta la amor del amich a moure son amat a pietat e a perdo abasta la amor del amat a donar a ses creatures gracia e benediccio

Si non sufficiat amor amici ad comovendum amatum suum ad pietatem et veniam? sufficiat igitur amor amati ad prestandum creaturis suis gratiam et benedictionem.

215. ¶ digues foll per qual cosa pots esser pus semblant a ton amat respos per entendre e amar de tot mon poder les fayçons de mon amat

Dic fatue per quod potes amato magis esse similis? qui respondit. intelligendo totis viribus intellectus mei decorem amati mei.

216. ¶ demanaren al amich si son amat havia defalliment de nulles coses e respos que hoch de [amadors *corrected in smaller hand*] loadors a honrar ses valors

Dic amice amatus tuus habetne defectum alicuius? qui respondit utique deficiunt ei amatores laudatores ad honorandum valores eius.

217. ¶ feria lamat lo cor de son amich ab vergues damor per ço que li fees amar larbre don lamat culli les vergues ab que fer sos amadors en lo qual arbre soferi mort e langors e [219r] desonors per restaurar a amor los amadors que perduts havia

Amatus virga amoris flagellabat cor amici. ut eum compelleret diligere arborem ex qua amatus virgas colligit quibus ferit amatores suos. in qua quidem arbore sustinuit amatus langores et obprobria nec non mortem ad restituendum amori amatores suos quos perdiderat.

213. The Lover kept vigils, fasted, wept, gave alms, and travelled in strange lands. All this was so that he could move the Will of his Beloved to inspire His subjects to honor His excellence.[126]

214. If the love of the Lover is insufficient to move his Beloved to pity and pardon, the love of the Beloved is enough to give His creatures grace and blessing.

215. "Say, fool, how can you be most like your Beloved?" He answered: "By understanding and loving with all my power the beauty of my Beloved."

216. They asked the Lover: "Does your Beloved lack anything?" He answered: "Yes, Lovers to praise and honor His excellence."

217. The Beloved beat the heart of the Lover with rods of love, in order to make him love the tree from which the Beloved cut the rods for beating His lovers. On that tree He suffered death, anguish, and dishonor to reclaim for love the Lovers that it had lost.[127]

---

126 The Lover's effort is necessarily insufficient, but not unsuccessful, as paragraph 214 explains.

127 The subject of "had lost" is presumably "love". Medieval exegesis often interprets rods more or less literally as metaphors for divine punishment or power, but also as images of the Word and of Christ's humanity, which Llull's usage here suggests. The tree is of course the Cross, so the rods (instruments from Christ's Passion) probably correspond to contrition generated by meditation on the Passion.

218. ¶ Encontra lamich son amat e viu lo molt noble e poderos e digne de tot honrament e dix li que fortment se maravellava de les gents qui tan poch lamaven el conexien el honraven com ell ne fos tan digne el amat li respos dient que ell havia pres molt gran engan en ço que havia creat home per ço quen fos amat conegut honrat e de mill homens los çent lo temien el amaven tant solament e de los çent los .xc. lo temien per ço que nols donas pena e los .x. lamaven per ço quells donas gloria e no era quaix quil amas per sa bonea e sa nobilitat Com lamich ohi aquestes paraules plora fortment en la desonor de son amat e dix amat qui tant has donat a home e tant las honrat per que home ha tant tu en ublit

Obviavit amicus amato suo viditque eum nobilem multum et potentem dignum omni honore et ait illi. miror de gentibus quia tam pauci cognoscunt diligunt et honorant te dignum omni amore. omni laude. omni honore. respondit amatus ei. fallor inquit non minime quod creavi genus humanum ut cognoscerer amarer et honorar[er *add. above line*] ab hominibus? de mille autem eorum centum me timent tantum. de ipsis vero centum me timent nonaginta ne penis eos affligam. de nonaginta. decem me diligunt ut dem eos frui perhempni gloria. Sed quasi nemo est qui me diligat propter bonitatem et nobilitatem meam. Quo audito planxit amicus lacrimabiliter super dedecus illatum amato suo et ait amate mi qui tanta homini tribuisti fecistique eum tam venerabilem quare te obliviscitur.

219. ¶ Loava lamich son amat e dehia que ell havia trespassat on cor ell es la on no pot atenyer on E per aço com demanaren al amich on era son amat respos es mas nos sabia on Empero sabia que son amat es en son remembrament

Laudabat amicus amatum suum dicens. tu amate mi transisti ubi. quia tu es. ubi nequit atingere ubi. Et ideo quando interrogabatur amicus ubi est amatus tuus? respondebat amicus. ipse est sed nescio ubi. scio tamen eum esse in memoratione mea.

220. ¶ Compra lamat ab sos honramens un home sclau e sotsmes a pensamens languiments suspirs e plors e demana li que menjava ni bevia Respos que ço que ell volia dena li que vestia respos que ço que ell volia dix lamat has gens de volentat Respos que serv e sotsmes no ha altre voler mas obeir a son senyor e son amat

Emit amatus honorificationibus suis servum et submisit eum cogitationibus. langoribus. suspiriis et fletibus. interrogavitque eum dicens. quid comedis et bibis? respondit servus ei domine comedo id quod vis. Iterum interrogavit eum quid induis? qui respondit. domine id quod vis. dixit amatus numquid habes aliquid voluntatis? qui respondit. servus inquid nullum habet aliud velle nisi obedire domino et amato suo.

221. ¶ demana lamat a son amich si avia [219v] paciencia Respos que totes coses li plahien e per aço no avia ab que agues pasciencia cor qui no avia senyoria en sa volentat no pudia esser inpacient
[Lacking in Latin text]

218. The Lover met his Beloved, and saw that He was very noble, powerful, and worthy of every honor. He told Him: "It astonishes me that people do not love, know, or honor you more, when you deserve all love, praise, and honor." The Beloved replied: "I was badly mistaken when I created people to love, know, and honor me. From every thousand people, only a hundred fear and love me. From that hundred, ninety fear me because I might punish them, while ten love me for the eternal glory I can give them, but hardly anyone loves me for my goodness and excellence." When the Lover heard these words, he wept hard at this dishonor to his Beloved. He said: "Beloved, you have given so much to people and honored them so much! Why have so many forgotten you?"

219. The Lover was praising his Beloved. He said He passed the bounds of space, because He exists beyond the reach of space.[128] So when they asked the Lover where his Beloved was, he answered: "He is, but no one knows where." Still, he knew that his Beloved was in his Memory.

220. The Beloved bought with His excellence a slave bound with cares, anguish, sighs, and tears. He asked: "What do you eat and drink?" The slave answered his lord: "Whatever you wish." He asked: "What do you wear?" It answered: "Lord, whatever you wish." The Beloved said: "Have you no Will of your own?" The slave answered: "A slave only wants to obey its master and Beloved."[129]

221. The Beloved asked His Lover if he was patient. He answered that he liked everything and so did not need patience, since people with no control over their Wills cannot be impatient.[130]

---

128 Literally, "where" or place, one of the ten categories or incidental characteristics of being in Scholastic metaphysics. Llull expresses the conventional theological argument that none of the categories apply to the divine being, but also presents this as a physical impossibility, which the mind overcomes through spiritual understanding.
129 The most extensive of several passages employing the Pauline image of the "slave of Christ" (1 Corinthians 7.22), bought through the Redemption. See also paragraphs 176, 243, 295, and 319.
130 That is, love controls the Lover's Will so completely that everything pleases him and nothing can make him impatient.

222. ¶ Amor se donava a quis volia e cor a molts homens nos donava e los amadors fortment no enamorava pus navia libertat per aço lamich damor se clamava e amor acusava a son amat mas amor sescusava dient que ella no era contra francha volentat per ço cor gran merit e gran gloria desirava a sos amadors

Amor cuicumque volebat se tribuebat. quoniam vero multis hominibus se non tribuebat nec vehementer philocapiebat amatores cum liber esset ad hoc conquerebatur amicus de eo accusans eum ad amatum suum. sed amor se excusans dicebat se non esse contra liberam voluntatem quia magnum meritum et magnam gloriam desiderabat amatoribus suis.

223. ¶ Gran contrast e gran discordia fo enfre lamich e amor per ço cor lamich sujava dels treballs que sostenia per amor e era questio si era per defalliment damor o del amich e vengren ne a jutjament del amat lo qual puni lamich ab languiment e guaardona lo ab muntiplicament damor

Magna obstantia magnaque discordia vertebatur inter amicum et amorem quia amicus fatigatus erat a laboribus quos propter amorem paciebatur. Et querebatur utrum hoc esset per defectum amoris vel amici. super hoc ambo ad iudicium amati venerunt qui punivit amicum langoribus tribuitque ei amoris multiplicationem.

224. ¶ Questio fo si amor era pus prop a pensament o a pasciencia Solve lamich la questio e dix que amor es engenrada en los pensaments e es sostentada en la pasciencia

Querebatur utrum amor propinquior esset cogitationibus quam pacientie vel pacientie [192vb] quam cogitationibus. amicus autem hanc questionem solvit dicens. amor generatur in cogitationibus et substentatur in pacientia.

225. ¶ Vehins del amich son los bells capteniments del amat e los vehins del amat son los pensaments de son amich e los treballs els plors que soste per amor

Vicine sunt amici speciose amati aptitudines. vicine vero amati sunt amici cogitationes tribulationes et fletus que amicus propter amorem sustinet.

226. ¶ Volch pujar molt altament la volentat del amich per ço que molt amas son amat e mana al enteniment que puyas a tot son poder el enteniment [que pujas deleted] ho mana al remembrament e tots .iii. puyaren contemplar lamat en sos honraments

Voluntas amici multum sublimiter voluit ascendere. ut multum diligeret amatum suum. mandavit intellectui ut totis viribus suis ascenderet intellectus hoc idem mandavit memorie. et omnes tres simul ascenderunt ad contemplandum amatum suum in honorificationibus suis.

222. Love gave itself to anyone it wished, but did not give itself to many people or inspire many strong Lovers, because this was its privilege. The Lover complained about love and criticized love to his Beloved. But love defended itself, saying it could not go against free will,[131] because it wanted more merit and glory for its Lovers.

223. A great argument and keen disagreement arose between the Lover and love, because the Lover was exasperated with the travails he endured for love. So the question arose: was this the fault of love or of the Lover? They went to seek judgement from the Beloved, and He punished the Lover with anguish and rewarded him with greater love.[132]

224. The question arose whether love was closer to cares or to patience. The Lover solved the problem: he said that love is born from cares and maintained through patience.

225. For neighbors the Lover has the beautiful ways of the Beloved. The Beloved has for neighbors the cares, travails, and tears that His Lover endures for love.

226. The Will of the Lover reached very high in order to love his Beloved more. It ordered the Intellect to reach up with all its power. The Intellect ordered the Memory to do the same. Together all three rose to contemplate the excellence of the Beloved.[133]

---

131 Although Llull always advocates an orthodox position regarding free will, it can appear difficult to reconcile this doctrine with his insistence on proving Christian beliefs through necessary reasons directed to the Intellect alone.

132 Paragraphs 223 through 225 all present dilemmas that illustrate the mutually interdependent relationship between love, the Lover, and the Beloved.

133 Llull always insists that the three powers of the soul seek spiritual perfection together (or "co-essentially," as he likes to say), without ever explaining exactly how this position accords with conventional doctrines, such as free will, that concern a specific power.

227. ¶ partis volentat del amich e donas al amat el amat mes en [220r] preso la volentat en lamich per ço que fos per ell amat e servit

Recessit voluntas ab amico et dedit se amato. amicus autem eam captam detinuit in amico ut per eum amaretur et honoraretur.

228. ¶ dehia lamich nos cuyt mon amat que jo sia departit a amar altre amat cor amor ma tot ajustat a amar un amat tant solament Respos lamat e dix nos cuyt mon amich que yo sia amat he servit per ell tant solament ans he molts amadors per qui som amat pus fortment [e *added above line*] pus longament que per samor

Dixit amicus ad amatum. amate mi non opinor a te me divisum esse ad diligendum alium amatum. quia amor me coniunxit totum ad diligendum unum solum amatum. respondit amatus non opinaris inquit amice mi me diligi a te solo et honorari. quia plures habeo diligentes me a quibus vehementius diligor et diucius quam a te.

229. ¶ dehia lamich a son amat amable amat tu has mos hulls acustumats e nudrits a veer e mes orelles a oir tos honraments E per aço es acustumat mon cor a pensaments per los quals has acustumat mos hulls a plorar e mon cors a languir Respos lamat al amich e dix que sens aytals custumes e nodriments no fora scrit en lo libre son nom en lo qual son scrits tots aquells qui venen a eternal benediccio e son delits lurs noms del libre on son scrits aquells qui van a eternal malediccio

Dixit amicus ad amatum suum amate mi dilectissime tu enutrivisti et erudisti oculos meos ad videndum et aures meas ad audiendum honores tuos introductus est ideo cor meum cogitationibus quibus instructi sunt flere oculi mei et languere cor meum. Respondit amatus amico dicens. non sine tali eruditione et introductione esset nomen tuum scriptum in libro ubi nomina eorum scribuntur qui perveniunt ad eternam benedictionem et ubi delentur nomina eorum qui corruunt in eternam maledictionem.

230. ¶ En lo cor del amich sajusten los nobles capteniments del amat e muntiplican los pensaments els treballs en lamich lo qual fora finit e mort si lamat muntiplicas en los pensaments del amich pus de sos honraments

Cordi amici adherent nobiles amati aptitudines. et multiplicantur in amico cogitationes et tribulationes. qui finitus esset et mortuus si amatus multiplicasset plus de honoribus in cogitationibus amici.

231. ¶ Vench lamat albergar al ostal de son amich e feu li son amich lit de pensaments e servien li suspirs e plors e paga lamat son ostal de remembraments

Venit amatus ad hospitandum in tabernaculum amici sui qui fecit ei lectum de cogitationibus. fletus et suspiria serviebant ei. amatus autem pro hospitagio solvit rememorationes.

227. The Will of the Lover left him and offered itself to the Beloved.[134] The Beloved imprisoned the Will in the Lover so that he would love and serve Him.

228. The Lover said: "My Beloved, don't worry about me leaving to serve another Beloved, because love has arranged for me to love only one Beloved." The Beloved answered: "My Lover, don't worry that you are the only one who loves and serves me, because I have many Lovers who love me harder and longer than you do."

229. The Lover said to his Beloved: "Dear Beloved! You have trained my eyes and ears to be accustomed to seeing and hearing your excellence. Likewise my heart is accustomed to caring, and this has accustomed my eyes to weeping and my body to languishing." The Beloved answered the Lover: "Were it not for this training and these habits, your name could not be written in the book that registers everyone destined for eternal blessing. Their names are deleted from the book that registers everyone destined for eternal damnation."[135]

230. The noble ways of the Beloved take hold in the heart of the Lover. They increase his cares and travail. He would die completely if the Beloved did not also increase His excellence in the thoughts of the Lover.[136]

231. The Beloved came to lodge at the inn of the Lover. The Lover made Him a bed of cares, and served Him longing sighs and laments. The Beloved paid His bill with memories.

---

134 The Will naturally seeks the good, in Scholastic psychology, and God is the Supreme Good.
135 The books of damnation and salvation from Revelation 20.11-15.
136 That is, love of God is always stronger than the travails that it brings.

232. ¶ Mescla amor los treballs els plaers en los pensaments del amich e clamaren se los plaers daquel mesclament e a[220v]cusaren amor al amant e feniren e deliren los plaers com lamat los hac departits dels turments que amor dona a sos amadors

Multiplicavit amor labores et placita in cogitationibus amici. placita vero conquerebantur ex illa commixtione et accusaverunt amorem ad amatum placita autem finita fuerunt et deleta postquam amatus segregavit ea a tormentis que amor infligit amatoribus suis.

233. ¶ los senyals de les amors quel amich ha a son amat son en lo començament plors e en lo mig tribulacions e en la fi mort e per aquells senyals lamich preyca los amadors de son amat

Signa amoris que facit amicus amato sunt in principio fletus. in medio tribulationes et in fine mors per hec autem signa predicat amicus amantibus amatum suum.

234. ¶ Asoliavas lamich e acompanyaven son cor pensaments e sos hulls lagremes e plors e son cors afliccions e dejunis e com lamich tornava en la companyia de les gents desemparaven lo totes les coses demunt dites e stava lamich tot sol enfre les gents

Stabat amicus solus. cor eius associabant cogitationes. et oculos eius fletus et lacrime et corpus eius iciuniorum afflictiones. dum enim amicus revertebatur in societatem gentium. omnia predicta derelinquebant eum tunc amicus solus morabatur inter gentes.

235. ¶ Amor es mar tribulada de ondes e de vents qui no ha port ni ribatge pereix lamich en la mar e en son perill perexen sos turments e nexen sos complimens

Amor est mare ventis et fluctibus agitatum carens omni portu et litore. periclitatur amicus in mari. in eius periclitatione tormenta sua pereunt et nascuntur complementa.

236. ¶ Digues foll que es amor Respos amor es concordança de tesorica e de praticcha a una fi a la qual se mou lo compliment de la volentat del amich per ço que faça a les gents honrar e servir son amat e es questio si la fi se cove pus fortment ab la volentat del amich qui desiga esser ab son amat

Dic fatue quid est amor? qui respondit amor est concordantia theorice et practice ad unum finem ad quem movetur complementum voluntatis amici ut faciat a gentibus amatum suum diligi et honorari

232. Love mixed travail and pleasure in the thoughts of the Lover. Pleasure complained about this confusion, and criticized love to the Beloved. But pleasure disappeared completely when the Beloved separated it from the travail that love gives to His Lovers.

233. The signs that the Lover loves his Beloved are longing sighs in the beginning, tribulations along the way, and death in the end. With these signs the Lover preaches to the Lovers of his Beloved.[137]

234. The Lover went off to be by himself. But his heart was accompanied by cares, his eyes by weeping and tears, and his body by affliction and fasting. When the Lover returned to be among people, all these things abandoned him, and the Lover was left all alone among the people.[138]

235. Love is a sea with violent winds and waves, but without any shore or harbor.[139] The Lover runs great risks at sea, but in this danger his torment dies and his final reward is born.

236. "Say, fool, what is love?" He answered: "Love combines theory and practice for a single ultimate purpose. This is the satisfaction that the Will of the Lover seeks, in order to make people honor and serve his Beloved." So the question arises: does this purpose belong most strongly to the Will of the Lover who desires to be with his Beloved?[140]

---

137 That is, preaching through deeds as well as words, a commonplace ideal of reforming movements in Llull's era.

138 The most explicit statement of another paradox of love, implied in several paragraphs: the Lover finds more company in his solitary anguish than in crowds of people.

139 Another pair of well-known Scriptural images, the sea of troubles and the safe harbor of salvation (Psalm 69.1-2, 107.23-30).

140 An application of the Lullian Relative Principle of Concord. The distinction between "theory and practice" is a commonplace of Scholastic philosophy. The concluding question (which does not appear in the Latin version) evidently asks whether a Lover devoted chiefly to being with the Beloved helps promote the goal of bringing others to know the Beloved.

237. ¶ demanaren al amich qui era son amat Respos que ço quil fahia amar desirar languir suspirar plorar scarnir murir

Dic amice quis est amatus tuus? respondit amicus. ille qui me facit diligere. desiderare. languere. suspirare. flere atque mori. [193ra]

238. ¶ demanaren al amat qui era son amich respos que aquell qui per honrar e loar sos honraments no duptava nulles coses e qui a totes coses renunciava per obeir sos manamens e sos consells
dic amate quis est amicus tuus? respondit amatus ille qui ad honorandum et laudandum honores meos nulla dubitat. et qui renunciavit omnibus ad obediendum mandatis et consiliis meis

239. [¶ *added*] digues foll qual feix es pus fexuch e pus greu [221r] o treballs per amor o treballs per desamor Respos que u demanas[en *deleted*] als homens qui fan penitencia per amor de son amat o per temor dels turments infernals

Dic fatue quid pondus magis grave est tolerari pro amore? aut labores aut odium? respondit amicus. ista queras ab hominibus penitentiam agentibus amore amati mei aut timore infernalium tormentorum.

240. ¶ Adurmis lamich e muri amor cor no ach de que visques despertas lamich e reviscola amor en los pensaments que lamich trames a son amat

Obdormivit amicus. mortuus est amor quia caruit unde viveret. evigilavit amicus vivificatus est amor in cogitationibus quas amato suo misit amicus.

241. ¶ dehia lamich que sciencia infusa venia de volentat devocio oracio e sciencia adquisita venia de estudi enteniment E per aço es questio qual sciencia es pus tost en lamich ni qual li es pus agradable ni qual es major en lamich

Dicebat amicus infusa scientia a studio provenit et ab intellectu. queritur que scientia citius provenit ad amicum et que magis grata est maiorque in amico.

242. ¶ digues foll don has tes necessitats Respos de pensaments e de desirar adorar treballar perseverança e don has totes aquestes coses respos damor e don has amor de mon amat e don has ton amat de si mateix tant solament

Dic fatue unde habes tibi necessaria. respondit amicus de cogitationibus. de desideriis de orationibus de tribulationibus et de perseverantia. unde habes [hec *in margin*] omnia? respondit amicus de amore. et unde habes amorem? de amato meo. et unde habes amatum tuum? respondit ex seipso.

237. They asked the Lover; "Who is your Beloved?" He answered: "The one who makes me love, desire, languish, sigh, weep, be mocked, and die."

238. They asked the Beloved: "Who is your Lover?" He answered: "The one who never hesitates to honor and praise my excellence, and who renounces everything for the sake of obeying my commandments and advice."

239. "Say, fool, which burden is harder and heavier, the travails of love or the travails of hate?" He answered: "Ask those who do penance from love for my Beloved and those who do it from fear of infernal punishment."

240. The Lover fell asleep and love died because it had nothing to live on. The Lover awakened and love revived from the thoughts sent by the Lover to his Beloved.

241. The Lover said that inspired knowledge came from the Will, devotion, and prayer, but that learned knowledge came from study and understanding. So the question arises: which knowledge is quicker, which is more pleasing, and which is greater in the Lover?[141]

242. "Say, fool, where do you get what you need?" He answered: "From caring, desiring, adoring, toiling, and persevering." "And where do you get all these things?" He answered: "From love." "And where do you get love?" "From my Beloved." "And where do you find your Beloved?" "All by Himself."

---

141 Since it poses the same kind of apparent dilemma expressed in so many other paragraphs, this question implies that both forms of knowledge are equally quick and pleasing. However, Llull frequently criticizes the curricula of the universities and claims that his own Great Art teaches the truth more quickly.

243. ¶ Digues foll vols esser franch de totes coses respos que hoc eceptat son amat vols esser catiu Respos que hoc de suspirs e pensaments treballs e perills e exils plors a servir mon amat al qual som creat per loar ses valors

Dic fatue vis ab omnibus esse liber? respondit utique excepto amato meo. vis esse servus? respondit utique suspiriis. cogitationibus. tribulationibus. periculis exiliis et fletibus . ut amato meo serviam. quia creatus sum ut magnificem valores eius.

244. ¶ turmentava amor lamich per lo qual turment plorava e planyia lamich cridaval son amat que sacostas a ell per ço que sanas On pus lamich a son amat sascostava pus fortment amor lo turmentava cor mes damor sentia e cor mes de plaers sentia on mes amava pus fortment lamat de sos languiments lo sanava

Tormentabat amor amicum. tormentis cuius plangebat cum fletu amicus. amatus eius clamabat ei dicens. amice mi accedas ad me et sanabo te. quanto plus ad amatum accedebat amicus tanto plus amor tormentabat eum. quia quanto plus amoris. tanto plus dulcedinis. sentiebat quanto plus diligebat. amatus a langoribus sanabat eum.

245. ¶ Malal[221v]ta era amor metjava lo lamich ab pasciencia perseverança obediencia sperança guarial amor en malaltia lamich sanava lo lamat donant li remembrament de ses virtuts e de sos honraments

Egrotabatur amor amicus medicabat eum pacientia perseverantia. spe et obedientia. amor convaluit. in amicum cecidit egritudo. amatus sanabat eum prestando ei suarum virtutum et decorum recordationem.

246. ¶ digues foll que es solitudo Respos solaç e companyia damich e amat e que es solaç e companyia [damic e amat *deleted*] respos que solitudo estant en coracge damich qui no membra mas tant solament son amat

Dic fatue quid est solitudo? respondit amicus solatia et societas amici et amati. que sunt solatia et societas? qui respondit. solitudo . existens in corde amici non recordantis nisi solum amati sui.

247. ¶ Questio fo feta al amich on es major perill en sostenir treballs per amor o benanançes acordas lamich ab son amat e dix que perills per malananςes son per impasciencia e perills per benanançes son per desconexença
amico questio facta fuit ubi maius esset periculum aut in sustinendo labores propter amorem aut beatitudines. concordavit amicus amato dicens. pericula in adversitatibus sunt per impacientiam pericula autem in beatitudinibus sunt per ingratitudinem.

243. "Say, fool, do you want to be freed from everything?" He answered yes, except from his Beloved. "You want to be a slave?" He answered: "Yes, to longing sighs, cares, travail, danger, exile, and weeping in order to serve my Beloved, because I was created to praise His excellence."[142]

244. Love tormented the Lover, and because of this torment the Lover wept and wailed. His Beloved called to him to come closer so that he could be cured. But the closer the Lover came to his Beloved, the more love tormented him, because he felt more love. But the more he loved, the more pleasure he felt, and so the Beloved cured his anguish even more.

245. Love was sick. The Lover administered medicines of patience, perseverance, obedience, and hope. Love recovered and the Lover became sick. The Beloved cured him by administering memories of His virtues and excellence.[143]

246. "Say, fool, what is solitude?" He answered: "The consolation and companionship of the Lover with the Beloved." "And what are consolation and companionship?" He replied: "Solitude in the heart of the Lover who remembers nothing but his Beloved."[144]

247. The Lover was asked a question: "Which poses the greatest danger: suffering travail for love, or happiness?" The Lover reached agreement with his Beloved, and answered that misery poses the danger of impatience, but happiness poses the danger of ignorance and ingratitude.

---

142 An expression of Llull's doctrine of the "first intention" (primary purpose) of every creature, which for humans is to serve, praise, love, and know God.

143 "Love was sick", that is, love weakened; "the Lover became sick", that is, with the anguish of renewed love.

144 This exclusive meditation on the Beloved perhaps corresponds to commonplace sufi doctrines regarding the soul's "passing away".

248. ¶ Solve lamat amor e licencia les gents quen prenguesen a tota lur volentat e apenes atroba amor qui la metes en son coratge E per aço plora lamich e ach tristicia de la desonor que amor pren çajus enfre nos per falses amadors e per homens desconexents

Solvit amatus amorem licentiavitque gentes ut eo tollerent ad libitum. vix invenit amor qui poneret eum in corde suo. ploravit ideo amicus et contristabatur propter dedecus quod amor infertur hic inter nos a falsis amantibus et ab ingratis hominibus.

249. ¶ Auçis amor en lo coratge de son vertader amich totes coses per ço que y pogues viure e caber e agra mort lamich si no agues membrança de son amat

Occidit amor in corde fidelis amici sui omnia. ut in eo recipi posset et vivere. Iam occidisset amicum nisi amati sui recordaretur.

250. ¶ havia en lamich dos pensaments la .i. cogitava tots jorns en la essencia e en les virtuts de son amat el altre cogitava en les obres de son amat E per aço era questio qual pensament era pus lugoros pus agradable al amat e al amich

Due cogitationes erant in amico. una quarum semper erat in essentia et in virtutibus amati sui. alia vero semper erat in operationibus amati sui. ideo queritur que duarum cogitationum erat splendidior magisque gratiosa amato et amico.

251. ¶ Muri lamich per força de gran amor soterral en sa terra lamat [222r] en la qual fo lamich resucitat e es questio lamich de qual reebe major do

Mortuus est amicus in fortitudine amoris maximi. amatus eum sepelivit in terram suam in qua amicus suscitatus est Queritur a quo susceperit maius donum.

252. ¶ En la preso del amat eren malanançes perills languimens desonors stranyedats per ço que no embaragasen son amich a loar sos honraments e a enamorar los homens qui lan en menyspreament

In amati carcere erant adversitates. pericula. langores. vituperia. alienationes. ut amicum non impedirent [193rb] laudare et magnificare amati honores ad philocapiendum homines a quibus spretus est.

253. ¶ Estava lamich .i. dia denant molts homens que son amat avia en est mon massa honrats per ço cor lo desonraven en lurs pensaments Aquells menyspreaven son amat e scarnien sos servidors plora lamich tira sos cabells bate sa cara e rompe sos vestiments e crida altament fo hanc fet tan gran falliment com menysprear mon amat

Stabat amicus quadam die coram multis hominibus quos amatus suus in mundo nimis honorificaverat quia in mentibus suis exprobrabant [cum *in margin*]. Isti autem spernebant amatum suum deridebantque servos eius. ploravit amicus erradicans capillos suos pre dolore. flagellabat faciem suam. delaniabatque vestimenta sua clamans alta voce dicens fuit unquam tanta iniquitas quanta est spernere amatum meum.

248. The Beloved freed love and let people accept it as they wished. But love hardly found anyone who would take it to heart. So the Lover wept and was sad because of the dishonor done to love by the false Lovers and ignorant people among us here below.

249. Love killed off everything in the heart of its true Lover in order to live there and fill it completely. The Lover would have died if he had not remembered his Beloved.[145]

250. Two cares occupied the Lover: first, he pondered every day the essence and virtues of his Beloved, and second, he pondered every day the works of his Beloved. So the question arose which care was most splendid and agreeable to the Beloved and to the Lover.[146]

251. The Lover died from the great power of love. The Beloved buried him in His land, where the Lover came back to life.[147] So the question arises: which most benefited the Lover?

252. The Beloved held captive adversity, danger, anguish, dishonor, and loneliness, so they would not prevent the Lover from praising His excellence and inspiring love in those who scorn Him.

253. One day the Lover stood before many people who had received so much worldly honor from his Beloved that now they thought little of Him. These people scorned his Beloved and ridiculed His servants. The Lover wept, pulled his hair, beat his face, ripped his clothes, and cried out loud: "Was any sin ever greater than scorning my Beloved?"

---

145 Compare similar themes in paragraphs 100 and 171.
146 That is, the Lover pondered the Creator's attributes in themselves and as manifested in the works of creation. These two focuses are fundamental to the entire system of Llull's Great Art, since its method consists in finding those attributes in all beings.
147 Perhaps to eternal life or to the life of the spirit (compare paragraphs 249 and 254).

254. ¶ digues foll vols murir respos que hoc en los delits daquest mon e en los
pensaments dels malehits qui ubliden e desonren mon amat en los quals pensamens
no vull esser entes ni volgut pus que no y es mon amat

Dic fatue vis mori? qui respondit utique in deliciis mundi et in cogitationibus
impiorum qui obliviscuntur et improbant amatum meum. in quorum mentibus nolo
esse nec intelligi quia amatus meus deest in eis.

255. ¶ si tu foll dius veritat seras per les gents ferit e scarnit repres turmentat e mort
Respos segons aytals paraules se segueix que si dehia falsies fos loat amat servit
honrat per les gents e defes dels amadors de mon amat

Si tu fatue veritatem protestaris? a gentibus quidem. flagellaberis. irrideberis.
reprehenderis. tormentaberis et occideris. qui respondit dicens secundum hec verba
sequitur ut si falsitatem protester laudabor diligar. magnificabor et honorabor a
gentibus et defendar a diligentibus amatum meum.

256. ¶ falses loadors blasmaven .i. dia lamich en presencia de son amat Ama lamich
pasciencia el amat justicia saviea poder el amich ama mes esser blasmat e repres que
esser negu dels falses blasmadors

Falsi laudatores quadam die amicum criminabantur in presentia amati sui. amicus
pacientiam habuit. et amatus iusticiam sapientiam et potestatem. amicus plus dilexit
increpari et reprehendi quam esse aliquis ipsorum false increpancium.

257. ¶ Sembrava lamat diversses sements en lo cor de son amich don nexia e fullava
e flo[222v]ria e granava un fruyt tant solament e es questio si daquel fruyt poden
nexer diversses sements

Seminabat amatus in cor amici sui diversa semina. unde oriebatur. frondebat et
florebat et granabat fructus quidam tantum. Queritur utrum ex illo fructu diversa
possint oriri semina.

258. ¶ Sobre amor esta altament lamat e dejus amor esta molt baxament lamich e
amor qui esta en lo mig devalla lamat a lamich e puja lamich a lamat e del
devallament e puyament viu e pren començament la amor per la qual langueix lamich
e es servit lamat

Super amorem existit amatus altissime. sub amore existit amicus infime. amor
autem qui consistit in medio facit amatum descendere ad amicum et amicum
ascendere ad amatum. ex hoc autem ascensu et descensu oritur et vivit amor per
quem languet amicus et servitur amato.

259. ¶ a la dreta part damor esta lamat e lamich esta a la sinestra E per aço sens que
lamich no pas per amor no pot pervenir a son amat

A dextris amoris sedet amatus. amicus vero a sinistris nisi autem amicus per
amorem transeat nequit ad amatum accedere

254. "Say, fool, do you want to die?" He answered: "Yes, to the delights of this world.[148] And likewise in the thoughts of the wicked who ignore and dishonor my Beloved, because I refuse to be understood or wanted in any minds where my Beloved is absent."

255. "Fool, if you tell the truth, people will beat, ridicule, criticize, torment, and kill you." He answered: "From that reasoning it follows that if I told lies, people would praise, love, and serve me and the Lovers of my Beloved would defend me."

256. One day flattering liars criticized the Lover in front of his Beloved. The Lover was patient and the Beloved was just, wise, and powerful. The Lover would rather be criticized and reprimanded, than be one of the lying critics.[149]

257. The Beloved planted several seeds in the heart of His Lover, and from these just one fruit sprouted, budded, flowered and ripened. So the question arises: will several seeds come from that fruit?

258. The Beloved is far above love, and the Lover is far below love. Between them, love brings the Beloved down to the Lover and lifts the Lover up to the Beloved. In this lowering and raising, love begins and lives. In this love, the Lover languishes and the Beloved is served.[150]

259. The Beloved stands on the right of love, and the Lover stands on the left. In this way, the Lover must pass through love to reach his Beloved.

---

148 A more obvious echo of the Pauline theme of "dying to the flesh" (Romans 8).

149 The identity of these critics is unclear, though some social or political comment is implicit. This paragraph interestingly applies to spiritual affairs the denunciation of flattery and mendacity often found in medieval literature on the evils of court society.

150 Another application of Llull's favorite scheme of contemplation as the ascent and descent of the soul, and the first of several paragraphs that suggest a trinitarian structure in the process of divine love.

260. E denant amor esta lamat e detras lamat esta lamich E per aço lamich no pot pervenir a amor tro que a passats sos pensaments e sos desirers per lamat
coram amore sedet amatus retro amatum sedet amicus. ideo amicus ad amorem nequit attingere quousque cogitationes sue et desideria transiverunt per amatum.

261. ¶ fa lamat a son amich dos semblants a si mateix amats en honraments e valors e enamoras lamich de tots tres egualment jassia que lamor sia una tant solament a significança de la unitat una en tres amats essencialment

Amatus amico producit duos similes sibi ipsi dilectis in valoribus et honoribus. amicus [autem *in margin*] omnes tres dilexit vehementer. licet amor sit unus tantum in significatione unius unitatis in tres amatos essentialiter.

262. ¶ vestis lamat del drap on era vestit son amich per ço que fos son companyo en gloria eternalment e per aço lamich desira tots jorns vermells vestiments per ço quel drap sia mills semblant als vestiments de son amat

Amatus pannum induit quo amicus indutus est ut amicus foret eius socius in eterna gloria. ideo amicus semper desideravit rubea vestimenta ut pannus suus sit amati sui vestimento similior.

263. ¶ digues foll que fahia ton amat ans quel mon fos respos covenias a esser per diversses proprietats eternals personals infinides on son amich e amat

Dic fatue quid agebat amatus tuus priusquam mundus esset? respondit amicus conveniebat eum esse in diversis proprietatibus eternalibus personalibus et infinitis ubi sunt amici et amati.

264. ¶ plorava e havia tristicia lamich com vehia a los infeels innorantment perdre son amat e ale[223r]gravas en la justiçia de son amat qui turmentava aquells quil conexien e li eren desobedients E per aço fo li feta questio qual era major o sa tristicia o sa alegrança ni si havia major benanança com vehia honrar son amat o major malenança com lo vehia desonrar

Lamentabatur amicus et tristabatur lacrimabiliter cum videret infideles perdere amatum suum. consolabatur autem in iusticia amati sui qui tormentis affligebat eos a quibus cognoscebatur nec ei fuerunt obedientes. ideo querebatur ab eo que maior erat aut tristicia aut leticia eius. et utrum maiorem haberet prosperitatem dum amatum honorari videret vel [maiorem *corrected from* amorem] adversitatem dum videret eum reprobari.

265. ¶ Esguardava lamich son amat en la major diferencia e concordança de virtuts e en la major contrarietat de virtuts e de vicis e en esser perfeccio quis covenen pus fortment sens defalliment e no esser que ab defalliment e ab no esser

Aspiciebat amicus amatum suum in maiori differentia et concordantia virtutum et in maiori contrarietate virtutum et vitiorum atque in esse perfectionis que sine defectu et non esse conveniunt vehementius quam cum defectu et non esse.

260. The Beloved stands in front of love, and the Lover stands behind the Beloved. In this way, the Lover cannot reach love unless his thoughts and desires have passed through the Beloved.

261. The Beloved makes for His Lover two Beloveds similar to Himself in excellence and worth. So the Lover falls in love with all three equally, but with one love. This signifies the essential unity of three Beloveds in one.[151]

262. The Beloved put on the clothes worn by His Lover so that the Lover would be His companion in eternal glory. So the Lover wishes every day for crimson clothes[152] that will make his clothing resemble more the clothing of his Beloved.

263. "Say, fool, what did your Beloved do before the world existed?" He answered: "It suited Him to exist through diverse eternal, personal, infinite properties, where the Lover and Beloved are."[153]

264. The Lover was sad and wept when he saw unbelievers who lost his Beloved without knowing it.[154] He rejoiced at the justice of his Beloved, when He tormented people who knew Him, but disobeyed Him. So the question arose: was he more sad or glad, and was he more blessed when he saw his Beloved honored or more unfortunate when he saw Him dishonored?

265. The Lover beheld his Beloved in the maximum difference and agreement between virtues, in the maximum contrast between virtues and vices, and in perfect being. These belong together more strongly without imperfection and non-being, than they would with imperfection and with non-being.[155]

---

151 In this explanation of veneration for the Trinity, Llull's use of the term "signifies" indicates well his method of treating all metaphysical and epistemological relationships as occasions for the perception of higher meanings.

152 Human flesh in general, but here probably martyrdom in particular.

153 An allusion to the heterodox doctrine of the eternity of the world, which Llull believed that "Averroist" philosophers were teaching at the University of Paris. The Lover's answer evidently means simply that God (and all three Persons of the Trinity) have existed eternally.

154 That is, have had no opportunity to know Christian doctrine.

155 A typical Lullian necessary reason, based on proportional affinities defined through his Relative Principles of Difference, Concord, Contrariety, and so forth.

266. ¶ Los secrets de son amat vehia lamich per diversitat concordança qui li revelaven pluralitat unitat en son amat per major conveniment de essencia sens contrarietat

Archana [193va] amati videbat amicus per diversitatem et concordantiam que pluralitatem et unitatem in amato suo revelabant amico. propter maiorem essentie convenientiam.

267. ¶ Digueren al hamich que si corrupcio qui es contra esser en ço qui es contra [esser *deleted*] generacio qui es contra no esser era eternalment corrumpent corrumput impossible cosa seria que no esser ni fi se concordas ab la corrupcio nil corrumput on per estes paraules lamich viu en son amat generacio eternal

Dictum fuit amico. si corruptio que [est *in margin*] contra esse eo quod est contra generationem existentem contra nonesse esset eternaliter corrumpens corruptum. impossibile esset nonesse et finem esse concordes corruptioni et corrupto. unde per hec verba amicus videbat in amato suo eternam generationem.

268. ¶ Si fos falsetat ço per que lamich pot mes amar son amat fora veritat ço per que lamich no pot tant amar son amat e si aço fos enaxi seguiras que defalliment fos de major e de veritat en lamat e agra en lamat concordança de falsetat e menor

Si id per quod amatum suum potest amicus plus diligere foret falsitas. foret enim veritas id per quod amicus amatum suum nequit tantum diligere. et si hoc ita esset sequeretur defectus maioris et veritatis in amato. essetque in amato concordantia falsitatis et minoris.

269. ¶.Loava lamich son amat e dehia que si son amat [223v] ha major possibilitat a perfecçio e mayor impossibilitat a inperfeccio cove que son amat sia simple pura actualitat en essencia e en operacio On dementre quel amich enaxi loava son amat li era revelada la trinitat de son amat

Magnificabat amatum suum amicus dicens. si amatus meus maiorem habet possibilitatem ad imperfectionem oportet eum esse puram et simplicem actualitatem in essentia et operatione. dum enim amicus amatum suum ita magnificaret. revelabatur ei amati sui trinitas.

266. The Lover saw the secrets of his Beloved through difference and agreement. These revealed to him plurality and unity in his Beloved, because they have the greatest essential agreement and no contrariety among them.[156]

267. They said to the Lover: If the degeneration opposed to being (because it opposes the generation opposed to non-being), were degenerating and degenerated forever, then it would be impossible for degeneration or the degenerated ever to converge with non-being or ending. From this argument the Lover sees that eternal generation exists in his Beloved.[157]

268. If the Lover were able to love his Beloved more through falsehood, then the Lover would love his Beloved less through truth. And if this were so, it would follow that imperfection coincided with superiority and truth in the Beloved, and that falsehood coincided with inferiority in the Beloved.[158]

269. The Lover praised his Beloved and said: "If my Beloved possesses the greatest possibility of perfection and the greatest impossibility of imperfection, then it follows that my Beloved is a single, pure actual being in both His essence and in His works."[159] While the Lover praised his Beloved in this way, the Trinity of his Beloved was revealed to him.

---

156 Another quintessentially Lullian necessary reason, based on relationships of self-evident "convenience" or agreement, expressed through his Relative Principles of Superiority, Concord, and so forth.

157 A necessary reason that attempts to prove the eternity of God by correlating the basic principles of being, non-being, generation, and degeneration, from Scholastic metaphysics and physics.

158 Which is absurd, so the assumption leading to this conclusion must be incorrect. The validity of this argument of course depends on accepting the correlations that Llull posits in the assumption.

159 An excellent example of how Llull invokes broad relationships from Scholastic metaphysics as necessary reasons for the Christian doctrine of the Trinity.

270. ¶ Vehia lamich en nombre de .i. e de .iii. major concordança que en altre nombre per ço cor tota forma corporal venia de no esser a esser per lo nombre demunt dit E per aço lamich esguardava la unitat e la trinitat de son amat per la major concordança de nombre

Videbat amicus in numero unius et trium maiorem concordantiam quia omnis forma corporalis de non esse veniebat ad esse per predictum numerum. ideo amicus unitatem amati sui aspiciebat per maiorem numeri concordantiam.

271. ¶ lamich loava lo poder el saber el voler de son amat qui havien creades totes coses enfora peccat lo qual peccat no fora sens lo poder el saber el voler de son amat [de son amat *deleted*] al qual peccat no son occasio lo poder nil saber nil voler de son amat

Laudabat amicus posse. scire et velle amati sui qui creavit omnia excepto peccato. quod non esset absque posse scire et velle amati sui cui etiam peccato non sunt occasio ipsa scilicet posse. scire et velle amati sui.

272. ¶ loava e amava lamich son amat com lavia creat e li havia donades totes coses e lohaval e amaval com li plac pendre sa semblança e sa natura e daço cove esser feta questio qual laor e amor deu haver major perfeccio

Laudabat et diligebat amicus amatum suum quia creavit eum et dedit ei omnia et maxime quia placuit amato sumere naturam amici et similitudinem. Queritur que laus et quis amor istarum laudum et istorum amorum debeant maiorem habere perfectionem.

273. ¶ Tempta amor lamich de saviesa e feu li questio si lamat lamava mes en pendre sa natura o en recrear lo el amich fo enbarbesclat tro que respos que la recreacio se covenc a esquivar malenança e la encarnacio a donar benanança e de la respunsio fo feta altra questio qual fo major amor

Temptavit amor amicum in sapientia querens ab eo utrum amatus plus eum diligeret accipiendo naturam et similitudinem eius quam in recreando ipsum vel e contrario. tunc amicus primo stupefactus erat usquequo respondit dicens. Recreatio convenit ad evitandum penam sed incarnatio ad largiendum beatitudinem Et ab hac responsione queritur iterum qui fuit maior amor.

274. ¶ Anava lamich demanar almoyna per les portes per ço que remembras la amor de son amat a sos servidors e per ço que [224r] husas de humiltat pobretat pasciencia qui son coses agradables a son amat

Ibat amicus per ianuas mendicando ut amorem amati sui servis eius denotaret et ut uteretur. humilitate. paupertate. et paciencia que sunt amato suo gratiosa.

270. The Lover saw in the numbers one and three greater agreement than between any other numbers, because anything with a bodily form came into existence from non-existence through these numbers.[160] Thus the Lover perceived the unity and trinity of his Beloved through this maximum numerical agreement.

271. The Lover praised the power, wisdom, and Will of his Beloved, who created everything except sin. Sin would not exist without the power, wisdom, and Will of his Beloved, and yet the power, wisdom, and Will of his Beloved did not cause sin.[161]

272. The Lover praised and loved his Beloved for creating and giving all things to him. He also praised and loved Him for choosing to take on his nature and likeness. So one must ask the question: which praise and love should be the most perfect?[162]

273. Love tested the Lover with a question about wisdom: Did the Beloved love him more when He took on his own nature[163] or when He created it anew? The Lover was baffled, but finally answered that the new creation was necessary in order to avoid misery, while the incarnation was necessary to provide happiness. This answer created another question: Which love was greater?

274. The Lover went begging from door to door in order to recall the love of his Beloved for His servants, and in order to practice the humility, poverty, and patience that please his Beloved.

---

160 Perhaps a reference to Llull's peculiar metaphysical doctrine of "innate correlatives", which attributes to every being the three essential constitutents of act, activity, and passivity.

161 A good illustration of the elementary catechetical instruction that Llull often provides in his works and perhaps suggestive of a concern for combating popular heresies, which he rarely mentions. Some heterodox groups held that the devil controlled sin or that another god had created evil.

162 The Lover's praise echoes the well-known phrase "in our image and likeness" from Genesis 1.26. The question apparently asks whether humans should be more grateful for their original creation or for their second creation through Christ.

163 That is, human nature. This paragraph compares the diverse benefits of the Incarnation and of the Resurrection (which recreated the human condition).

275. ¶ demanaren perdo al amich per amor de son amat el amich no tant solament perdona ans los dona si meteix e sos bens

Querebatur ab amico propter amorem amati sui venia. amicus non solum eis contulit veniam ymo potius semetipsum et bona sua dedit eis.

276. ¶ ab lagremes de sos hulls recontava lamich la passio e la dolor que son amat sostench per samor e ab tristicia pensaments scrivia les paraules que dehia e ab misericordia sperança se conortava

Occulorum suorum lacrimis recitabat amicus passionem et dolorem quem amatus suus amore ipsius amici sustinuit. cum tristicia et cogitationibus recitata scribebat. misericordia et spe se consolabatur.

277. ¶ lamat e amor vengren veer lamich qui durmia lamat crida a son amich e amor lo desperta el amich obey a amor e respos a son amat

Amatus et amor venerunt ad videndum amicum qui dormiebat. clamavit amatus amicum. respondit amor amato.

278. ¶ Nudria lamat son amich a amar e amor ensenyava li a perillar e pasciencia ladoctrinava com sostengues treballs per la amor daquell a qui ses donat per servidor erudiebat amatus amicum suum diligere. amor docebat eum subire pericula. paciencia instruebat eum tribulationes sustinere amore illius qui pro servo se tribuit.

279. ¶ demanava lamat a les gents si havien vist son amich e ells mostraven li les calitats de son amich el amat dix que son amich era ardit temeros ric e pobre alegre trist consiros e languia tots jorns per samor

Interrogabat amatus gentes numquit vidistis amicum meum? illi autem ostendebant qualitates amici eius. Inquit amatus eis. amicus meus erat audax et timidus. dives et pauper. letus et tristis et considerosus. amore mei semper languit.

280. E demanaren al hamich si volia vendre son desirer e ell respos que venut lavia a son amat per .i. tal diner que tot lo mon ne poria esser comprat

Et interrogabatur amicus. vis amice vendere desiderium tuum? respondit amicus. vendidi inquit desiderium meum amato meo precio illius denarii a [193vb] quo totus orbis emi posset.

281. ¶ preycha foll e digues paraules de ton amat plora dejuna renuncia al mon lamich e ana cerchar son amat ab amor e loava lo en aquells lochs on era desonrat

Predica fatue dic de amato tuo sermones. lacrimare et ieiunia. renuntiavit mundo amicis et ivit querendo amatum suum cum amore et magnificabat eum ubi reprobabatur.

275. They asked the Lover to pardon them, out of love for his Beloved. The Lover not only pardoned them, he gave them himself and his belongings as well.

276. With tears in his eyes, the Lover described the Passion and suffering that his Beloved endured for his love. Sadly and pensively he wrote out the description he composed.[164] And he comforted himself with mercy and hope.

277. The Beloved and love came to see the Lover while he was sleeping. The Beloved called to His Lover, and love awakened him. The Lover obeyed love and answered his Beloved.[165]

278. The Beloved trained his Lover to love, love showed him how to face danger, and patience taught him how to endure travail for love of the one whose servant he had become.

279. The Beloved asked people: "Have you seen my Lover?" They asked Him the qualities of His Lover.[166] He said: "My Lover is daring, fearful, rich, poor, happy, sad, and thoughtful. He languishes every day with love for me."

280. They asked the Lover: "Would you sell your desire?" He said: "I have sold my desire to my Beloved for the price that would buy the whole world."

281. "Preach, o fool, and talk about your Beloved! Weep! Fast!" The Lover rejected the world, went looking for his Beloved with love, and praised Him wherever He was dishonored.

---

164 Just as Blanquerna the Hermit wrote the *Book of the Lover and the Beloved*. Many of Llull's shorter treatises perhaps resulted from applying the contemplative methods of his Great Art to particular topics.

165 A simple allegory of the human response to grace in general and in particular of the response to God that any well-ordered soul must make, according to Llull.

166 This translation makes more sense than the Catalan and Latin texts: "They showed the qualities of the Lover to Him."

282. ¶ Bastia e obrava lamich una bella ciutat on estegues son amat ab amor pensaments plants [224v] plors e languiments la obrava e ab plaers sperança devoçio la ornava e ab fe justicia prudencia fortitudo temprança la guarnia

Amicus amoribus. cogitationibus planctibus lacrimis. et langoribus edificabat civitatem in qua amatus eius habitaret. placitis. spe. devotione ornabat eam. fide autem iusticia. prudentia fortitudine et temperantia muniebat eam.

283. ¶ Bevia lamich amor en la font de son amat en la qual lamat lava sos peus a son amich qui moltes vegades ha ublidats menyspreats sos honramens per que lo mon es en defalliment

Potabat amicus in fonte amati sui in quo amatus pedes amici lavit qui sepissime reprobavit honores eius. quare mundus est in defectu.

284. ¶ digues foll que es peccat Respos entencio girada e enverssada contra la final entencio e raho per que mon amat ha creades totes coses
[Lacking in Latin]

285. ¶ Vehia lamich quel mon es creat com sia cosa que eternitat se covenga mills ab son amat qui es essencia infinida en granea e en tota perfeccio que ab lo mon qui ha cantitat finida E per aço en la justicia de son amat vehia lamich que la eternitat de son amat cove esser devant ha temps e a quantitat finida

Intellexit amicus mundum esse creatum eo quod eternitas melius amato suo convenit que est essentia infinita in magnitudine et in perfectione quam mundo quantitas cuius finita est. Idcirco intellexit amicus in iusticia amati sui quod eternitatem amati sui oportet presse tempori et quantitati finite.

286. ¶ Escusava lamich son amat a aquells qui dehien quel mon es eternal dient que son amat no hagra justicia perfeta si no retes a cascuna anima son cors a lo qual no fora bastant loch ni materia ordial nil mon no fora [bastant *deleted*] ordenat a una fi tant solament si fos eternal e si no u fos defallira en son amat perfeccio de volentat saviea

Excusabat amicus amatum suum eis qui mundum affirmabant esse eternum dicens. amatus meus perfectam non haberet iusticiam nisi unicuique anime corpus suum redderet cui locus non sufficeret nec materia ordinalis nec etiam mundus ordinatus esset ad unum finem tantum si foret eternus. et nisi ad unum ordinatus esset deficeret in amato meo perfectio sapientie et voluntatis.

282. The Lover laid out and built a beautiful city where his Beloved could live amidst love, care, laments, weeping, and anguish. He decorated it with pleasures, hope, and devotion. He furnished it with faith, justice, prudence, fortitude, and temperance.[167]

283. The Lover drank love from the fountain of his Beloved, where the Beloved washed the Lover's feet. The Lover has often forgotten and scorned His excellence and so the world is in disorder.[168]

284. "Say, fool, what is sin?" He answered: "Any purposes turned and twisted against the final purpose or reason for which my Beloved created all things."[169]

285. The Lover saw that the world is created, since eternity necessarily pertains more to his Beloved (who is essentially and infinitely great and perfect) than it does to the world (which is finite in quantity). So from the justice of his Beloved the Lover saw that the eternity of his Beloved must precede time and finite quantity.[170]

286. The Lover defended his Beloved to those who claimed that the world is eternal. He argued that his Beloved would not be perfectly just if He did not return a body to every soul, but there was not enough space and prime matter for this.[171] Likewise, the world would not be established for one purpose alone if it were eternal, and if it were not established for one purpose, then his Beloved would not be perfect in Will and wisdom.

---

167 The city is clearly the Lover's soul, a meaning given by medieval exegetes to the "city set on the hill" of Matthew 5.14.

168 Literally, "in default" or "defective". Llull probably refers to the disorder caused by sin, a doctrine especially developed by Anselm and often invoked in Llull's writings.

169 Again, a reference to Llull's doctrine of first and second "intentions", which broadly assumes Anselm's doctrine of the right order of creation.

170 Paragraphs 285 and 286 offer more of Llull's "necessary reasons" for refuting the Parisian "Averroists" who advocate the heterodox doctrine of an eternal universe.

171 That is, the number of souls would eventually exceed the amount of material available for furnishing them with bodies at the Last Judgement.

287. ¶ digues foll en que has conexença que la fe catholica sia vera e la creença dels
jueus e dels sserrayns sia en falsetat e error Respos en les .x. condicions del libre del
gentil e dels tres savis

Dic fatue in quo cognoscis fidem catholicam esse veram? et ea que iudei et
sarraceni credunt esse in errore et falsitate. respondit amicus in decem conditionibus
libri gentilis et trium sapientium.

288. ¶ digues foll en que comença saviea Respos en fe e en devocio qui son scala on
puja [225r] lenteniment entendre los secrets de mon amat e fe e devocio don han
començament Respos de mon amat qui inlumena fe e scalfa devocio

Dic fatue in quo incipit sapientia? respondit amicus. in fide et devotione que sunt
scala per quam ascendit intellectus ad archana amati mei. dic? fides et devotio unde
habent principium? respondit amicus de amato meo qui fidem illuminat et
devotionem calefacit

289. ¶ demanaren al amich qual cosa era major o possibilitat o inpossibilitat Respos
que possibilitat era mayor en creatura e inpossibilitat en son amat con ssia cosa que
possibilitat e potencia se concorden e impossibilitat e actualitat

Querebatur ab amico que maior esset aut possibilitas aut impossibilitas. respondit
amicus dicens. possibilitas maior est in creatura sed impossibilitas maior est in
amato meo cum impossibilitas et actualitas conveniant possibilitas vero et potentia.

290. ¶ digues foll qual cosa es major o diferencia o concordança Respos que fora
son amat diferencia era major en pluralitat e concordança en unitat mas en son amat
eren eguals en diferencia e unitat

Dic fatue que maior est aut differentia aut concordantia. Respondit amicus. extra
amatum meum est differentia maior in pluralitate et concordantia maior in unitate sed
in amato meo sunt equales distinctio et concordantia in pluralitate et unitate

291. ¶ digues amador que es valor Respos que lo contrari de la valor daquest mon la
qual es desirada per los falses amadors vanaglorioses qui volen valer havents
desvalor e per esser perseguidors de valor

Dic amator quid est valor. Qui respondit oppositum valoris mundi qui a falsis
amatoribus et ab eis quos inanis gloria vexat diligitur qui valere volunt dedecus
paciendo ad essendum valoris persecutores.

287. "Say, fool, how do you know the Catholic Faith is true and what the Jews and Muslims believe is false and wrong?" He answered: "From the ten conditions in the *Book of the Gentile and Three Sages.*"[172]

288. "Say, fool, where does wisdom begin?" He answered: "In faith and devotion: they are the ladder ascended by the Intellect in order to understand the secrets of my Beloved." "And where do faith and devotion begin?" He answered: "In my Beloved: He gives the light of faith and fire of devotion."

289. They asked the Lover: "Which is greater, possibility or impossibility?" He answered: "Possibility is greater in a creature, but impossibility in my Beloved. This is because possibility and potential existence coincide, just as impossibility and actual existence do."[173]

290. "Say, fool, which is greater, difference or agreement?" He answered: "Outside my Beloved, difference is greater in plurality and agreement is greater in unity, but within my Beloved they are equal in plurality and unity."[174]

291. "Say, Lover, what is worthiness?" He replied: "The opposite of the worthiness in this world that false Lovers and the vainglorious seek. They desire worthiness while being unworthy because they persecute worthiness."[175]

---

172 One of Llull's writings, in which a pagan hears a debate among representatives of Christianity, Islam, and Judaism.
173 Another necessary reason created from the correlation of basic logical and metaphysical principles. Llull means that impossibility and actuality coincide in God because it is impossible for the divine nature to be more or other than it already actually is.
174 That is, the Trinity does not involve the kind of difference or plurality found in creatures.
175 Paragraphs 291-93 all deal with the true nature of various social virtues. Llull's explanation of these virtues typically consists in an interpretative play of opposites: false mundane vices contrastively imply true divine virtues.

292. ¶ digues foll has vist home qui sia orat Respos que ell havia vist un bisbe qui avia a sa taula molts enabs e moltes scudelles e talladors dargent e havia en sa cambra moltes vestedures e gran lit e en ses caxes molts diners e a la porta de son palau havia pochs pobres

Dic fatue vidisti aliquem hominem insensatum? Qui respondit. vidi inquit quendam episcopum habentem ad mensam suam plures ciphos et cupas multasque scutellas et cissoria argenti. habebat etiam in camera plurimas vestes preciosas. eius quidem cubile longum [erat *in margin*] et amplum multum. nec non eius arche et gazophylatia referta denariis. pauci autem pauperes ad portas palacii eius erant expectantes.

293. ¶ foll sabs que es viltat Respos vils pensamens e que es leyaltat temor de mon amat nada de caritat e de vergonya qui tem blalme de les gents e que es honrament respos cogitar mon amat e desirar e loar sos honraments

Scis fatue quid est vilitas? qui respondit. viles cogitationes. et quid est legalitas? respondit timor amati mei ortus ex karitate et ex verecundia que a gentibus formidat increpationes. Quid est honor? respondit cogitare de amato meo et desiderare et magnificare laudem et honorem eius.

294. ¶ los treballs e les tribulacions quel hamich sostenia per amor lalteraren e lenclinaren [225v] a impaciencia e repres lo lamat ab sos honramens e ab sos prometiments dient que poch sabia damor qui salterava per maltrets ni per benanança Ach lamich contricçio e plors e prega son amat que li retes amors

Labores et tribulationes que sustinebat amicus propter amorem alterabant eum et inclinabant eum ad impacientiam. reprehendit amatus [194ra] eum suis honoribus et promissionibus dicens. amice pauca scis [amoris *in margin*] qui per adversitates et beatitudes alteraris? amicus contrictionem habuit cum lacrimis oravitque amatum suum dicens amate mi redde mihi amores.

295. [¶ *inserted*] foll digues que es amor Respos que amor es aquella cosa qui los franchs met en servitut e a los serfs dona libertat e es questio a qual es pus prop amor o a libertat o a servitut

Dic fatue quid est amor? qui respondit amor est id quod liberos in servitutem convertit et servos in libertatem Queritur quid propinquius sit amori [*corrected from* amoris] aut libertas aut servitus.

296. ¶ Cridava lamat son amich e ell li responia dient quet plau amat qui est hulls de mos hulls e pensaments e compliment de mos compliments e amor de mes amors e encara començament de mos començaments

Clamabat amatus amicum suum. respondit amicus ei dicens ecce adsum amate mi quid tibi placet. tu qui es oculus oculorum meorum et mens mentis mee et complementum complementorum meorum etiam principium principiorum meorum?

292. "Say, fool, have you seen any crazy person?" He replied: "I have seen a bishop who put many silver goblets, bowls, and knives on his table, many clothes and a big bed in his room, and much money in his purse. But he allowed few poor people around the door of his palace."[176]

293. "Fool, do you know what villainy is?" He answered: "Villainous thoughts." "And what is loyalty?" "Fear of my Beloved, which is born from love and the shame that fears the criticism of others." "What is honor?" He replied: "Meditating on my Beloved, desiring and praising His excellence."

294. The travail and tribulation that the Lover endured for love disturbed him and made him impatient. But the Beloved scolded him with His excellence and promises, saying that anyone affected by misery or happiness knew little about love.[177] The Lover wept with contrition and begged his Beloved: "Oh my Beloved, return love to me."

295. "Say, fool, what is love?" He answered that love is what makes free people slaves and slaves free. So the question arises: is love closer to freedom or to slavery?

296. The Beloved called his Lover, and he answered Him saying: "Here I am, my Beloved, what is your pleasure? You are the eye of my eyes, the thought of my thoughts, the satisfaction of my satisfactions, and above all the foundation of my foundations."[178]

---

176   Notice that this mundane craziness contrasts with the divine foolishness of the Lover.
177   That is, the Lover must display constancy in love, regardless of the travails or joys that love brings.
178   The first of several passages employing repetitive word-play, which Llull often uses to suggest conceptual and real relationships. The Beloved's call and the Lover's reponse echoes Scriptural scenes concerning a divine summons. Analogies with God's call to the patriarchs or prophets--such as Abraham (Genesis 22.1), Jacob (Genesis 46.2), Moses (Exodus 3.4), Samuel (1 Samuel 3.4-8), or Isaiah (Isaiah 6.8)--especially suggest a prophetic role for the Lover, as noted in regard to paragraph 334.

297. ¶ Amat dehia lamich a tu vaig e en tu vaig cor mapelles Contemplar vaig contemplacio en contemplacio ab contemplacio de ta contemplacio En ta virtut so e ab ta virtut vench don prench vertut Salut te ab ta salutacio qui es ma salutacio en ta salutacio de la qual esper salutacio perdurable en benediccio de ta benediccio en la qual beneit som en ma benediccio

A mate mi dixit amicus ad te vado. in te vado quia vocas me. vado ad contemplandum contemplationem in contemplatione. In virtute tua sum. cum virtute tua venio ex qua virtutem accipio. te saluto cum salutatione tua et in salutatione tua ex qua spero salutem perpetuam in benediccione benedictionis tue in qua benedictus sum in benedictione mea.

298. ¶ Alt est amat en tes altees a les quals exalçes ma volentat exalçada en ton exalçament ab ta altea qui exalça en mon remembrament mon enteniment exalçat en ton exalçament per conexer tos honraments e per ço que la volentat naja exalçat enamorament e la memoria naja alta remembrança

S ummus es amate mi in altitudine tua ad quam exaltas voluntatem meam et exaltatam in exaltatione tua cum altitudine que in comemoratione mea exaltat meum intellectum et exaltatum in exaltatione tua ad cognoscendum honores tuos ut voluntas mea exaltatam habeat philocaptionem et exaltatam memoria recordationem.

299. [¶ *inserted*] Gloria est amat de ma gloria e ab ta gloria en ta gloria dones gloria a ma gloria qui ha gloria [226r] de ta gloria per la qual tua gloria me son gloria egualment los treballs e los languiments quim venen per honrar ta gloria ab los plaers els pensaments quim venen de ta gloria

A mate mi tu es glorie mee gloria cum omni gloria in gloria tua largiris gloriam glorie mea que gloriam habet a gloria tua. per quam gloriam tuam sunt equaliter mihi gloria tribulationes et langores que insurgunt adversum me ad honorandum gloriam tuam cum placitis et dulcibus cogitationibus que de gloria tua mihi adveniunt.

300. ¶ Amat en lo carçre damor me tens enamorat ab tes amors qui man enamorat de tes amors per tes amors e en tes amors cor als no est mas amors en les quals me fas estar sol e ab companyia de tes amors e de tos honraments Car tu est sol en un sol qui som solitari ab mos pensaments com la solitat tua sola en honors maja sola a loar e honrar ses valors sens temor dels desconexents qui no tan sol en lurs amors

A mate mi in amoris carcere me philocaptum detines cum tuis amoribus qui de tuis amoribus me philocapere per tuos amores et in amoribus tuis quia nihil aliud est preter amores in quibus stare solum me compellis in amorum consortio et honorum tuorum quia tu solus es in me solo existente solitario in cogitationibus meis. cum solitudo tua sola in honoribus sola me faciat honorare et magnificare valores suos absque ingratuitorum formidine qui te solum non habent in amoribus suis.

297. "Beloved," said the Lover, "I am going to you and I am going in you, because you are calling me. I am going to contemplate contemplation in your contemplation, with your contemplation, and from your contemplation. I am in your virtue, I am coming to your virtue, and I am coming with your virtue, from which I get virtue. I greet you with your greeting, which is my greeting in your greeting. From this I hope for eternal salvation[179] in the blessing of your blessing. And in this I am blessed in my blessing."

298. "Beloved, you are high in your height.[180] You exalt my Will there, exalted in your exaltation with your height. In my Memory this exalts my Intellect, exalted in your exaltation, to know your excellence. So from this my Will has exalted loving and my Memory exalted remembering."

299. "You are the glory, Beloved, of my glory. With your glory and in your glory, you give glory to my glory, which glories from your glory. This glory of yours makes the travail and anguish that I get from honoring your glory equally glorious to me, along with the pleasures and cares that I get from your glory."

300. "Beloved! You hold me in love with your love in the prison of love. It has made me fall in love with your love, through your love, and in your love. You are nothing but love, and this keeps me alone in the company of your love and excellence. You alone are solely in me, as I sit with my solitary cares, while your singly excellent solitude[181] alone keeps me praising and honoring your worthiness, without any fear of the ignorant who do not love you alone."

---

179 A pun created from the similarity between the words for "salutation" and "salvation".
180 Probably in the sense of "most high" or "most exalted" ("highest of the high").
181 That is, the Beloved's complete possession of the Lover's attention.

301. ¶ Solaç est amat de solaç per que en tu [a *written above line*] solaç mos pensaments ab ton solaç qui es solaç e confort de mos languiments e de mes tribulacions qui son tribulades en ton solaç con no asolaçes los innorants ab ton solaç e com los conexents de ton solaç no enamores pus fortment a honrar tos honraments

Tu es amate me solatiorum solatium quare mens mea habet in te solatium qui es solatium langorum meorum et tribulationum mearum in solatio tuo. idcirco langores mei multiplicantur nam agnoscentes solatium tuum in te non habent solatium vehementius ad honorandum honores tuos.

302. ¶ Clamavas lamich a son senyor de son amat e a son amat de son senyor dehien lo senyor e lamat qui fa en nos departiment qui som una cosa tant solament Responia lamich e dehia que pietat de senyor e tribulacio per amat

Conquerebatur amicus domino suo de amato suo. et amato suo de domino suo qui dixerunt. qui facit in nobis divisionem qui tantum unus idem sumus. respondit amicus pietas domini et tribulatio propter amatum.

303. ¶ perillava lamich en lo gran pelech damor e confiavas en son amat qui li acurria ab tribulacions pensaments lagremes e plors suspirs e languiments per ço cor lo pelech era damors e de honrar ses honors [226v]

Periclitabatur amicus in maxima pelvi amoris. confidebat enim in amato suo qui cum tribulationibus. cogitationibus. lacrimis. suspiriis. fletibus et langoribus succurrebat ei quia pelvis erat amori et reverencie honorum suorum.

304. ¶ Alegravas lamich cor era son amat cor per son esser es tot altre esser sdevengut e sostentat e ubligat e sotsmes a honrar servir lesser de son amat qui per null esser no pot esser delit ni encolpat ni minvat ni crescut

Letabatur amicus quia amatus suus est. esse cuius est omne aliud esse et devenit et et sustentatur et obligatur atque sumitur ad honorandum et serviendum esse amati mei quod a nullo esse deleri potest nec inculpari nec minui nec augeri.

305. ¶ Amat en la tua granea fas grans mos desirers e mos pensaments e mos treballs Cor tant es gran que tota res es gran que de tu a membrança e enteniment e plaer e ta granea fa poques totes coses qui son contra tos honraments manaments

Amate mi in magnitudine tua magnificas. desidera cogitationes et labores meos. quia tam magnus es quod omne magnum est quod de te habet memorationem intellectum et placitum. magnitudo tua omnia parvificat que sunt contra honorificationes tuas et mandata tua.

306. ¶ Eternalment comença e ha començat e començara mon amat e eternalment no comença ni ha començat ni començara e aquests començaments no son contradiccio en mon amat per ço cor es eternal e ha en si unitat e trinitat

Eternaliter [194rb] incepit. incipit et incipiet amatus meus. nec eternaliter incepit. nec incipit. nec incipiet. hec autem inceptio et non inceptio non contrariantur in amato meo quia eternus est in trinitate et unitate sua.

301. "Beloved, you are the consolation of consolations, because I console my cares in you with your consolation. It consoles my anguish and comforts my tribulation. Your consolation causes travail when you do not console the ignorant with your consolation and do not make those who do not know your consolation more desirous to honor your excellence."

302. The Lover complained to his Lord about his Beloved, and to his Beloved about his Lord. The Lord and the Beloved said: "Who is trying to divide us this way, when we are one and the same?" The Lover answered: "The pity of the Lord and tribulation for the Beloved."

303. The Lover faced danger on the great sea of love, but trusted in his Beloved. He rescued him with tribulations, worries, tears, weeping, sighs, and anguish, because this sea was for love and honoring His excellence.

304. The Lover rejoiced that his Beloved existed. Through His existence all other existence came to be, is maintained, and is bound and obliged to honor and serve the existence of the Beloved.[182] Nothing that exists can erase, inhibit, decrease, or increase His existence.

305. "Beloved! You make my desires, my cares, and my travail great in your greatness. This is because you are so great that everything becomes great when it remembers, understands, or enjoys you. Your greatness makes anything opposed to your excellence and commandments small."[183]

306. "My Beloved eternally begins, has begun, and will begin. He eternally does not begin, has not begun, and will not begin. These beginnings are not contradictory in my Beloved, because He is eternal and has in Himself unity and trinity."

---

182 This is the Lullian "first intention" of every creature.
183 Paragraphs 305 through 312 are evidently meditations on the Lullian Absolute Principles of Goodness, Greatness, and so forth.

307. ¶ Lo meu amat es .i. e en sa unitat sunexen en una volentat mos pensaments e mes amors e la unitat de mon amat abasta a totes unitats e a totes pluralitats E la pluralitat qui es en mon amat abasta a totes unitats e pluralitats

Amatus meus unus est atque in unitate sua uniuntur in una voluntate cogitationes mee. amoresque mei. unitas autem amati mei omnibus unitatibus et pluralitatibus sufficit. atque pluralitas que in amato meo est omnibus unitatibus et pluralitatibus sufficit.

308. ¶ Subira be es lo be de mon amat qui es be de mon be cor es be mon amat sens altre be cor si no ho fos mon be fora daltre be subira e cor no ho es sia doncs tot lo meu be despes en esta vida ha honrar lo subira be cor enaxi cove

Summum bonum est bonum amati mei quod est bonum boni mei quia amatus meus est bonum absque alio summo bono. quia nisi ita esset. bonum meum foret ex alieno summo bono. Sed quoniam hoc nequit esse. ergo omne bonum meum in hac vita exponatur ad honorandum suum bonum quoniam ita oportet.

309. ¶ Si tu amat sabs mi peccador sit fas tu piados e perdonador e cor ço que sabs en tu es mellor que mi [227r] doncs jo se en tu perdo e amor pus que tu fas saber a mi contriccio e dolor e desirer de pendre mort per loar ta valor

Si tu amate mi scis me miserum peccatorem. fac te pium et misericordem. et quoniam id quod in te scis melius est quam id quod in me scio. ergo scio in te veniam· et amorem cum me scire facias mihi contrictionem dolorem et desiderium sustinendi mortem pro valore tuo.

310. ¶ lo teu poder amat me pot salvar per benignitat pietat e perdo e pot me dampnar per justicia e per colpes de mos fallimens complescha ton poder ton voler en mi cor tot es compliment sia quem don[s *erased*] salvacio o dampnament

Potestas tua amate mi me salvare potest per benignitatem pietatem et veniam. potest etiam me dampnare per iusticiam propter culpas delictorum meorum. perficiat potestas tua in me velle tuum quia totum est perfectio licet mihi des salvationem aut dampnationem.

311. ¶ Amat veritat visita la contriccio de mon cor e puya aygua a mos hulls com ma volentat la ama e cor la tua veritat es subirana puja veritat çajus ma volentat a honrar tos honraments e devalla la a desamar mos defallimens

Amate mi contrictionem cordis mei visitat veritas et ascendit aqua ad oculos meos dum mea voluntas eam diligit. Et quoniam veritas tua summa est. extollit veritas voluntatem meam hic inferius ad honorandum honores tuos et declinat eam ad odiendum delicta mea.

307. "My Beloved is one. In His unity my cares and desires unite as one Will. The unity of my Beloved upholds all unities and pluralites, and the plurality in my Beloved upholds all unities and pluralities." 184¡

308. "The Sovereign Good is the good of my Beloved, and He is the good of my good. This is because my Beloved is good without any other good: were He not, my good would come from some other sovereign good. But this cannot be, so it is right that all my worldly goods should be spent on honoring the Sovereign Good."

309. "Beloved, if you know me to be a sinner, then have pity and mercy on me. What you know in yourself is better than I am. So I know pardon and love in you, because you make me know contrition, pain, and the desire to face death to praise your worthiness."

310. "Beloved, your power can save me through goodness, pity, and mercy. It can damn me through justice and the guilt from my sins. Let your power fulfill your Will in me, because whether you save me or damn me, it will be fulfilled all the same."

311. "Beloved! When my Will loves truth, this brings contrition to my heart and tears rise up in my eyes. Because your truth is supreme, truth raises my Will to honor your excellence and lowers it to reject my sins."185

---

184 A relationship most obvious in Llull's theory of "innate correlatives": these are three essential features of act, activity, and passivity that he attributes to all creatures, thus making them reflections of their triune Creator.

185 This passage again recalls the contemplative ascent and descent through which the soul seeks the Creator's truth in creatures. Llull's almost exclusively moral and spiritual concept of that truth (suggested here by its association with contrition and sin) helps explain his fierce opposition to the theology and philosophy of the schools.

312. ¶ Anc ver no fo ço en que mon amat no fo e fals es ço en que mon amat no es e
fals sera ço en que mon amat no sera E per aço de necessitat es que sia veritat tot
quant sera ni fo ni es si mon amat hi es E per aço fals es qui es en ver on mon amat
no es sens que no sen segueix contradiccio

Non fuit verum ubi amatus meus non fu[it *added above line*] falsum est ubi amatus
meus non est. et falsum erit ubi amatus meus non erit ergo necessario oportet verum
esse omne quod fuit. omne quod est. et omne quod erit si amatus meus sit et fuerit
in eo. ideo falsum est omne quod est in vero ubi amatus meus non est. nec tamen
sequitur contradictio.

313. ¶ Crea lamat e destrui lamich jutja lamat plora lamich Recrea lamat gloria al
hamich feni lamat sa operacio e romas lamich eternalment en companyia de son amat
Creavit amatus et destruxit amicum. Iudicavit amatus ploravit amicus. Recreavit
amatus gloriam amico. terminavit amatus operationem suam. remansit amicus
eternaliter in eternali consortio amati sui.

314. ¶ per les carreres de vegetacio e de sentiment e de ymaginacio e de enteniment
volentat anava lamich cerchar son amat en aquelles carreres havia lamich perills e
languiments per son amat per ço que exalças son enteniment e sa vo[227v] a son
amat qui vol quels seus amadors lentenen el aman altament
Per vias vegetationis sensus et ymaginationis atque intellectus et voluntatis ibat
amicus querendo amatum suum. In illis autem viis sustinebat amicus pericula et
langores propter amatum ut intellectum suum et voluntatem suam exaltaret ad
amatum qui vult ut amatores sui eum intelligant et diligant excellenter.

315. ¶ Mou se lamich a esser per lacabament de son amat e mou se a no esser per
son defalliment E per aço es questio qual dels .iii. moviments han mayor
apoderament en lamich naturalment
Amicus se movet in esse per perfectionem amati sui et se movet in nonesse per
defectum suum. ideo queritur quis duorum motuum maiorem habeat naturaliter
potestatem in amico.

316. ¶ posat mas amat enfre mon mal e ton be a la tua part sia pietat misericordia
pasciencia humilitat e perdo ajuda e restaurament a la mia part sia contriccio
perseverança membrança ab suspirs lagremes e plors de la tua santa passio
Amate mi tu posuisti me inter bonum tuum et malum meum. ex parte tui sint
pietas. misericordia. paciencia. humilitas. venia adiutorium et restauratio. ex parte
vero mei sint contrictio et perseverantia et tue sancte passionis recordatio suspiriis et
fletibus cum dulci fonte lacrimarum

312. "Nothing was ever true unless my Beloved was there, anything is false unless my Beloved is there, and anything will be false unless my Beloved is there. Everything that will be or was or is necessarily must be true if my Beloved is there. Therefore anything true is false without my Beloved, and no contradiction follows from this."[186]

313. The Beloved created and the Lover destroyed. The Beloved judged and the Lover wept. The Beloved created glory anew for the Lover. The Beloved completed His work and the Lover remained forever in the company of his Beloved.[187]

314. The Lover went to find his Beloved through the paths of nourishing, sensing, imagining, understanding, and willing.[188] On those paths the Lover faced danger and anguish for his Beloved, in order to raise his Intellect and Will to his Beloved. The Beloved wishes His Lovers to understand and love Him highly.[189]

315. The Lover comes to exist through the perfection of his Beloved, and ceases to exist because of his sin. So the question arises: which of these two processes is by nature more powerful in the Lover?

316. "Beloved, you have set me between my evil and your good. On your side, let there be pity, mercy, patience, humility, pardon, help, and renewal; on my side, let there be contrition, perseverance, and remembering, with longing sighs, tears, and weeping for your holy Passion."

---

186 A compelling general statement of Llull's view that all knowledge depends on God. The mention of past, present, and future times probably alludes in particular to Scholastic logical doctrines regarding the temporal qualification of true and false propositions.
187 A neat allegory of the Fall, Redemption, and Salvation.
188 That is, the levels of the human soul as defined by Llull, from the lowest (nourishment) to the highest (mind).
189 That is, God should be the highest object of both knowledge and desire for the human soul. This dual objective constitutes Llull's somewhat facile solution to the difficult problem of defining the relationship between faith and reason and between the operations of Will and Intellect.

317. ¶ Amat quim fas amar si nom ajudes per quem volguist crear ni per que per mi portest tantes langors ni sostenguist tan greu passio pus tant mas ajudat a exalçar ajudam amat a devallar a membrar airar mes colpes e mos defallimens per ço que mills mos pensaments pusquen pujar a desirar honrar loar tes valors

O dilecte qui me facis diligere. nisi mihi auxilieris quare creasti me. quare pro me tantos tulisti langores tantamque sustinuisti pro me passionem? postquam autem auxiliatus es ad exaltandum me. Amate mi auxiliare mihi ut descendam ad odiendum culpas et delicta mea ut melius ascendere valeam ad honorificandum et laudandam valorem tuum.

318. ¶ Mon voler has fet franch a amar tos honraments e ha menysprear tes valors per ço que pusques a mon voler muntiplicar tes amors

Amate [194va] mi velle meum fecisti liberum ad amandum honores tuos et ad spernendum valores tuos ut ipsi velle meo multiplicare possis amores tuos.

319. ¶ En aquesta libertat has amat perillada ma volentat Amat en aquest perill deus remembrar ton amich qui de sa volentat francha trau servitut a loar tes honors e a muntiplicar en son cors languimens e plors

In hac quidem libertate exposuisti voluntatem meam periculo. amate mi in hoc periculo digneris amici tui reminisci ut a libertate voluntatem suam in servitutem convertas magnificandum honores tuos et ad multiplicandum in corde eius langores fletus et suspiria.

320. ¶ Amat hanc de tu en ton amich no vench colpa ni falliment ni en ton amich compliment sens ton do e perdo e doncs pus lamich [228r] ta en aytal possessio nol hages en hublit en ses tribulacions ni en son perillament

Amate mi de te nunquam venit culpa nec defectus in amicum nec in eo complementum absque munere tuo et venia. ergo quia amicus tuus in talem te habet posessionem non obliviscaris eum in tribulationibus suis nec in periculis suis.

321. ¶ Amat qui en .i nom est nomenat hom e deu en aquell nom ihesu crist te vol ma volentat home e deu E si tu amat has tant honrat ton amich sens los merits en nomenar e voler ton nom per que no honres tants homens innorables qui cientalment no son estats tan colpables al teu nom ihesu crist com es stat lo teu amich

Amate mi qui uno nomine deus et homo diceris in ipso nomine ihesu christi te desiderat voluntas mea deum et hominem tu autem amate mi quia amicum tuum absque suis meritis honorificasti nominando et volendo hoc tuum nomen quare plurimos homines ignorantes non honorificas qui scienter non sunt tantum nomini tuo jhesu christo culpabiles quantum fuit amicus tuus.

317. "Beloved, you make me love! If you will not help me, why did you choose to create me? Why did you bring me so much anguish and suffer such a cruel Passion? Now that you have helped me ascend so high, Beloved, help me descend to remember and hate my guilt and sins, so that my thoughts can rise better to desire, honor, and praise your worthiness."

318. "You have made my Will free to desire your excellence or scorn your worthiness, in order to increase your love in my Will."[190]

319. "Beloved, you have endangered my Will with this freedom. Beloved, please remember your Lover in this danger! He accepts slavery with a free will in order to praise your excellence and to increase anguish in his heart, weeping, and longing sighs."

320. "Beloved! No guilt or sin ever came to your Lover from you, and no virtue ever filled your Lover without your grace and pardon. So, since the Lover can only possess you in this way, do not forget him in his tribulations or danger."

321. "Beloved, one name calls you man and God! My Will longs for you as man and God in that name, Jesus Christ. Beloved, since you have favored your unworthy Lover so greatly in naming and desiring your name, will you favor as well all those ignorant people who, unlike your Lover, do not know the wrong they commit against your name Jesus Christ?"[191]

---

190 Paragraphs 318 and 319 offer an especially concise statement of the doctrine of free will, as understood by Llull.
191 That is, the unbelievers who do not recognize the Incarnation, the union of humanity and divinity indicated in the name "Jesus Christ".

322. ¶ Plorava lamich e dehia a son amat aquestes paraules Amat no fuist avar ni cobeu al teu amich en donar esser ni en recrear lo ni en donar li moltes creatures a son serviy doncs don vendria amat que tu qui est subirana libertat ffosses avar a ton amich de plors pensaments languiments Saviea e amors a honrar tes honors E per aço amat lo teu amich te demana vida longa per tal que puscha reebre de tu molts dels dons demunt dits

Plorabat amicus dicens amato suo hos sermones. amate mi nunquam cupidus nec avarus fuisti adversus amicum tuum dando ei esse et recreando eum subdendo quam plurimas creaturas servicio eius ergo unde contingeret amate mi qui es summa libertas te esse avarum amico tuo fletibus cogitationibus. langoribus sapientia et amore ad magnificandum honores tuos. ideo amatus tuus dierum longitudinem a te deposcit ut multa predictorum munerum suscipere possit.

323. ¶ Amat si tu ajudes als homens justs de lurs mortals enemichs Ajuda a muntiplicar mos pensaments en desirar tes honors E si tu ajudes als homens injusts com recobren justicia ajuda al teu amich com faça de sa volentat sacrifiçi a ta laor e de son cors a testimoni damor per via de martire

Si tu amate mi iustis auxilieris adversus mortales inimicos eorum. auxiliare mihi ad multiplicandum cogitationes meas ut desiderem honores tuos. Et si iniustis auxilieris ut in iusticiam convertantur auxiliare amico tuo ut de voluntate sua faciat sacrificium laudi tue et de corpore suo amoris testimonio per viam martirii.

324. ¶ No ha mon amat diferencia en humilitat humil humiliat cor tot es humilitat en pura actualitat E per aço lamich repren erguyll qui vol pujar a son amat aquells qui en est mon la humilitat de mon amat a tant honrats [228v] e ergull los ha vestits de ypocresia vanagloria vanitats

Non habet amatus meius differentiam in humilitate quia totum est humilitas in pura actualitate ideo reprehendit amicus superbiam volentem ad amatum suum extollere eos qui in mundo humilitatem amati sui magnificaverunt superbia enim in vanitate induit eos ypocrisim et inanem gloriam.

325. ¶ humilitat ha humiliat lamat al hamich per contriccio e sis feu per devocio e es questio en qual damdues lamat fos pus fortment humiliat a lamich

Humilitas amatum humiliavit amico per contrictionem et etiam per devotionem. Queritur in qua harum duarum humiliatus est vehementius amatus amico.

326. ¶ Ach lamat per sa perfeccio misericordia de son amich e si sach per les necessitats de son amich e fo questio per qual de les dues rahons lamat perdona pus fortment les colpes de son amich

Propter perfeccionem suam habuit amatus misericordiam in amico suo et etiam propter necessitatem ipsius amici. Queritur per quam harum duarum rationum parcit amatus cicius amico suo.

322. The Lover wept and said these words to his Beloved: "Beloved! You were never stingy or greedy with your Lover in making the creation, in recreating it, or in providing him with many creatures to serve him. So why is it, supremely generous Beloved, that you have become stingy with your Lover when it comes to tears, cares, anguish, wisdom, and love for honoring your excellence? Your Lover must ask you for a long life in order to receive all these gifts from you."

323. "Beloved! Since you help the just against their mortal enemies, help my thoughts to desire your excellence. Since you help the unjust to find justice, help your Lover to sacrifice his Will for your praise and his body as testimony to love through martyrdom."

324. "There is no difference between humility, the humble, and humiliation[192] in my Beloved, because He is completely and purely actualized humility. This is why the Lover criticizes pride, and seeks to draw toward his Beloved those people whom the humility of my Beloved has honored so greatly in this world. Pride has clothed them in hypocrisy, vainglory, and vanities."

325. Humility has humbled the Beloved to the Lover through contrition, and likewise through devotion. So the question arises: which of these two ways humbled the Beloved most completely to the Lover?

326. The Beloved had mercy on the Lover because He is perfect, and likewise on account of the needs of the Lover. The question arose: which of these was a stronger reason for the Beloved to pardon the sins of His Lover?[193]

---

192 These three terms suggest the Lullian "innate correlatives", although the Latin version mentions only the first. The exact connection between this metaphysical distinction and the moral lesson that follows is somewhat obscure.

193 In Llull's theology and metaphysics, God's "perfection" implies fullness and completion, while humankind's "needs" imply lack and imperfection. Thus the question poses a dilemma: God's perfection and humankind's imperfection are equally compelling "reasons" for divine pardon.

327. ¶ Pregaven nostra dona e los angels els sants de gloria mon amat e com remembre la error en quel mon es per desconexença membre gran la justicia de mon amat e gran la desconexença de sos enemichs

Virgo dei genitrix et omnes angeli omnesque sancti celestis glorie amatum meum orabant. cumque recolerem errorem in quem mundus per ingratitudinem volvitur recordatus sum iusticie amati mei et ingratitudinis inimicorum suorum

328. ¶ pujava lamich los poders de sa anima per scala de humanitat gloriejar la divina natura e per la divinal natura devallava los poders de sa anima per gloriejar en la humana natura de son amat

Elevabat amicus potestates anime per scalam humanitatis ad glorificandum divinam naturam et per divinam naturam declinabat potestates anime sue ad glorificandum in humana natura amatum suum.

329. ¶ On pus estretes son les vies on lamich va a son amat pus amples son les amors e on pus stretes son les amors pus amples son les vies e per aço en totes maneres a lamich per son amat amors e treballs e languimens e plaers e consolacions

Quanto vie sunt arciores per quas amicus tendit ad amatum suum. tanto laciores sunt amores. Etiam amores quanto sunt artiores tanto sunt vie latiores. ideo propter amatum fert omnimode amicus. amores tribulationes. langores placita et consolationes

330. ¶ Hixen amors damors e pensaments de languiments e plors de languiments e entren amors en amors e pensaments en plors e languiments en suspirs el amat sguardas son amich qui a per sa amor totes aquestes tribulacions

Procedunt amores ex amoribus. cogitationes ex lango[194vb]ribus et lacrime ex cordis suspiriis et amores intrant in amores et cogitationes in fletus et langores in suspiria. amatus speculatur amicum amore sui gerentem has omnes tribulationes.

331. ¶ Trenuytaven e fahien romeries e pele[229r]grinacions los desirers els remembraments del hamich en les noblees de son amat e aportaven al amich fayçones e umplien son enteniment de resplandor per la qual la volentat muntiplicava ses amors

Agebant peregrinationes desideria et rememorationes amici in nobilitatibus amati sui. gerebantque ipsi amico decorem et pulcritudinem et adimplebant intellectum suum splendoribus per voluntatem multiplicabantur amores illius.

332. ¶ lamich ab sa ymaginacio pintava e formava les fayçons de son amat en les coses corporals e ab son enteniment les pulia en les coses sperituals e ab volentat les adorava en totes creatures

Amicus per ymaginem suam pingebat et formabat in corporalibus domibus decoras formositates amati sui. Intellectu spirituales domos poliebat. cum voluntate adorabat eum in omnibus creaturis.

327. "Our Lady, the angels, and the saints in glory prayed to my Beloved. When I remembered the error that exists in the world from ignorant ingratitude, I remembered how great is the justice of my Beloved and how great the ignorant ingratitude of His enemies."[194]

328. The Lover raised the powers of his soul through the stages of human nature, in order to glorify the divine nature. He lowered the powers of his soul through divine nature, in order to glorify the human nature of his Beloved.[195]

329. Where the paths by which the Lover seeks his Beloved are narrowest, the love is widest. And where the love is narrowest, the paths are widest. This is why in every way the Lover bears love, travail, anguish, pleasure, and consolation for his Beloved.[196]

330. Love springs from love, cares from anguish, and tears from a sighing heart. Love merges into love, cares into tears, and anguish into sighs. The Beloved beholds His Lover accepting all these tribulations for the sake of His love.

331. The desires and memories of the Lover spent the whole night travelling on a pilgrimage to the excellences of the Beloved.[197] They brought beauty to the Lover and filled his Intellect with splendor. Thanks to this his Will grew in love.

332. The Lover shaped and pictured in his Imagination the lovely features of his Beloved from corporeal things. With his Intellect he polished them in spiritual things. With his Will he adored them in all creatures.[198]

---

194 These probably include both unbelievers and those Christians who impede the spread of the Faith.
195 That is, the Lover's soul contemplated the glory of Christ's divinity and humanity, using Llull's favored methods of ascent and descent through the levels of being.
196 That is, the Lover necessarily experiences both joy and pain in love.
197 That is, in a vigil of contemplation.
198 A concise explanation of how the soul should use material data provided by the Senses and Imagination in order to understand spiritual truths through the Intellect and Will.

333. ¶ Compra lamich un dia de plors per altre dia de pensaments e vene un dia damors per altre de tribulacions e muntiplicaren ses amors e sos pensaments

Uno die amicus de fletibus. in alio vero die de cogitationibus. uno die vendidit amicus de amoribus in alio vero die de tribulationibus et multiplicati sunt eius amores et tribulationes

334. ¶ Era lamich en terra stranya e ublida son amat e enyoras de son senyor e sa muller e sos infants e de sos amics mas retorna remembrar son amat per ço que fos consolat e que la sua stranyedat no li donas enyorament ni marriment

Stabat amicus in terra aliena et oblitus est amatum suum. anxiebatur de domino de uxore de filiis et de amiciis suis. reversus ad se [amicus *in margin*] amatum suum recoluit ut consolaretur et ne alienitas sua anxietatem inferret ei nec dolorem.

335. ¶ hoyia lamich paraules de son amat en les quals lo vehia son enteniment per ço cor la volentat havia plaer daquell ohiment e lo remembrament membrava les virtuts de son amat e los seus prometiments

Audiebat amicus sermones amati sui in quibus intellectus suus videbat eum quia voluntas in auditu ipsorum delectabatur et in recordatione ipsorum recordabatur virtutum amati sui et promissionum eius

336. ¶ Ohia blasmar lamich son amat en lo qual blasme vehia lenteniment la justicia e la paciencia de son amat cor la justiçia punia los blasmadors e la pasciencia los esperava a contriccio penediment E per aço es questio en qual dels dos lamich crehia pus fortment

Audiebat amicus amatum suum reprobari in hac quidem reprobatione aspiciebat intellectus iusticiam et pacientiam amati sui quia iusticia reprobantes puniebat pacientia vero expectabat eos ad contrictionem et penitentiam. Queritur in qua duarum habebat amicus maiorem fiduciam.

337. ¶ Malalt fo lamich e feu testament ab consell de son amat [colpes e torts lexa *in smaller hand*] [229v] a penediment penitencia [e delits temporals *in smaller hand*] lexa a menyspreament a sos hulls lexa plors e a son cor suspirs e amors e a son enteniment lexa les fayçons de son amat e a son remembrament la passio que sostench per samor son amat e a son negoci lexa lendreçament dels infeels qui innorantment van a perdiment

Egrotabatur amicus et condidit testamentum consilio amati sui. legavit enim culpas et iniurias contritioni et penitentie. legavit delicta temporalia sperniciei. et occulis suis fletus et cordi suo suspiria et amores et intellectui suo decorem et iucunditatem amati sui et memorie sue passionem quam amatus suus amore sui sustinuit. et negociis suis distribuit et legavit directionem infidelium qui ignoranter in perpetuum subeunt perditionem.

333. The Lover bought one day of weeping with another day of cares. He sold one day of love for another day of tribulations. Both his love and his cares grew.

334. The Lover was in a strange land: he forgot his Beloved, and longed for his lord, his wife, his children, and his friends.[199] But he returned to remembering his Beloved so he would be consoled and so his loneliness would not cause homesickness or melancholy.

335. The Lover heard words from his Beloved. His Intellect saw Him in them because his Will was pleased by what it heard. Then his Memory remembered the virtues and promises of his Beloved.

336. The Lover heard criticism of his Beloved. In that criticism his Intellect saw the justice and patience of his Beloved, because justice punished the critics and patience waited for their contrition and penitence. So the question arises: which of these did the Lover believe in most strongly?

337. The Lover became sick and made out his last will and testament with the advice of his Beloved. He left sins and wrongs to penance and penitence and earthly delights to scorn. He left tears to his eyes, longing sighs and love to his heart, the impression of his Beloved to his Intellect, and the Passion that his Beloved suffered for love to his Memory. To his business he left the task of guiding the unbelievers who unknowingly risk damnation.[200]

---

199 Perhaps not a missionary journey abroad, but the "foreign realm" of mundane affairs. This echo of Moses's expression "stranger in a strange land" (Exodus 2.22) may reflect Llull's view of himself as a kind of prophet to a captive people, a role that his *Life* certainly ascribes to him.

200 That is, those who have never had the opportunity to hear God's word.

338. ¶ Odora lamich flors e remembra pudors en rich avar e en lucxurios e en desconexent ergullos Gusta lamich dolçors e entes amargors en les possessions temporals e en lenteniment e hiximent daquest mon Senti lamich plaers temporals el enteniment entes lo breu trespassament daquest mon e en los perdurables turments als quals son occasio los delits qui a aquest mon son agradables

Odoravit amicus flores recoluit fetores in divite avaro et in luxurioso atque in ingratuito superbo gustavit amicus dulcedinem et in amaritudinibus temporalibus atque in ingressu mundi senciit temporalia placita Intellectus intellexit breves mundi transitus necnon in perpetuis suppliciis quibus sunt ocasio delicie mundi que mundanis hominibus voluptuose sunt

339. ¶ hac lamich fam set calor e fret pobretat nuedat malaltia tribulacio e fora finit si no hagues membrança de son amat quil sana ab sperança remembrament e ab lo renunciament daquest mon e ab lo menyspreament del blasme de la gent

Amicus paciebatur esuriem. sitim. calorem. frigus. paupertatem. egritudinem. tribulationes. Iam finitus esset amicus nisi in memoria portaret amatum qui sanavit eum spe. rememoratione et renuntiatione deliciis mundanis atque in spretu reprobationum gentium.

340. ¶ Enfre treball e plaer era lo lit del amich ab plaer sadurmia e ab treball se despertava e es questio a quals de aquests dos es pus prop lo lit del amich

Inter labores et placita erat lectus amici. in placitis dormiebat. in laboribus evigilabat. Queritur quid istorum duorum propinquius esset lecto amici.

341. ¶ En va sadurmi lamich cor temia lo blasme de la gent e despertas en pasciencia com remembra laors de son amat e es questio lamich de qui ach major vergonya o de son amat o de les [230r] gents

In ira obdormiebat amicus formidabat enim reprobationes gentium. evigilabat amicus in paciencia dum recordatus est corporis amati sui. Queritur de quo plus verecundabatur amicus aut de amato aut de gentibus.

342. ¶ Cogita lamich en la mort e ach paor tro que remembra la çiutat de son amat de la qual mort e amor son portals e entrament

Cogitavit amicus de morte fuitque perterritus usquequo recoluit civitatem amati sui cuius sunt mors et amor portalia et ingressus.

343. ¶ Clamavas lamich a son amat de temptacions qui li venien tots jorns treballar sos pensaments el amat li respos dient que temptacions son occasio com hom recorra ab remembrament remembrar deu e amar sos honrats cabteniments

Conquerebatur amicus amato de temptationibus que per singulos dies veniebant ei turbantes [195ra] cogitationes suas. Inquit amatus ei. Temptatio est occasio recurrendi cum rememoratione ad rememorandum deum et diligendum decoras nobilitates eius.

338. The Lover smelled some flowers: from this he remembered the stink of a rich miser, a lecher and a proud fool. The Lover tasted sweet things: from this he understood the bitterness of worldly possessions and of the way we enter and leave this world. The Lover felt worldly delights: from this his Intellect understood our short journey through this world and how the pleasures that delight people in this world cause eternal torment.[201]

339. The Lover was hungry, thirsty, hot, cold, poor, naked, and in trouble. He would have died had he not remembered his Beloved, who healed him with hope, remembrance, rejection of this world, and scorn for the criticisms of other people.

340. The Lover made his bed between agony and pleasure: he fell asleep with pleasure and awakened in agony. The question arises: which of these is closest to the bed of the Lover?[202]

341. The Lover went to sleep angry, because he disliked how people criticized him. He woke up feeling patient when he remembered the praises of his Beloved. So the question arises: who made the Lover feel most ashamed, his Beloved or the people?

342. The Lover meditated about death. He felt fear until he remembered the city of his Beloved,[203] to which death and love are the gates and entrance.

343. The Lover complained to his Beloved about the temptations that came every day and disturbed his mind. The Beloved answered that temptations provide an opportunity for using the Memory to recall God and to love His beautiful excellence.

---

201 An excellent example of the broadly moralizing interpretation that guides most Lullian argumentation. Here, each material thing symbolizes some contrary spiritual truth.
202 Paragraphs 340 and 341 perhaps offer an allegory of the "bed of conscience" and "sleep of spiritual torpor" (compare the imagery in paragraphs 28, 103, 240, 277 and 345).
203 That is, eternal life, using the image of the heavenly Jerusalem from Hebrews 11.10-16 or Revelation 21.

344. ¶ Perde lamich una joya que molt amava e foras desconsolat tro que son amat li feu questio qual cosa li era pus profitable o la joya que havia o la pasciencia que hac en les obres de son amat

Perdidit amicus clenodium valde dilectum ei. Iam desolatus esset donec amatus eius questionem obiecit ei dicens. amice quod est tibi utilius aut clenodium quod habuisti prius aut pacentia quam in operibus amati tui sustines?

345. ¶ durmia lamich considerant en los treballs e ls empacxaments los quals ha en servir son amat e hac pahor que ses obres no perissen per aquells empacxaments mas lamat li trames consciencia quil desperta en sos merits e en los poders de son amat

Obdormiebat amicus considerans in impedimentis et laboribus que tolerandus erat serviendo amato suo. timuitque ne sua perirent opera per impedimenta. Amatus autem conscienciam misit amico que in meritis et in potestatibus amati sui excitavit eum.

346. ¶ Avia lamich [a *written above line*] anar longues carreres e dures e aspres e era temps que anas per aquelles e que portas lo gran feix que amor fa portar a sos amadors E per aço lamich aleuja sa anima dels pensaments els plaers temporals per ço quel cors pugues portar lo carrech pus leugerament el anima anas per aquelles carreres en companyia ab son amat

Amicus iturus erat longas duras et asperas vias. tempus enim erat ut per eas pergeret ferens pondus maximum quod amor ab amatoribus suis ferri compellit. Ideo amicus animam suam a temporalibus cogitationibus et desideriis alleviavit ut corpus hoc pondus posset sustinere levius et anima per has vias pergeret ab amato suo sociata.

347. ¶ Denant lamich dehien .i. jorn mal de son amat sens quel amich no y respos ni scusa son amat e es questio qual es pus encolpat ols homens qui blasmaven lamat ol amich qui callava e no scusava [230v] son amat

Quadam die homines obloquebantur amato in conspectu amici Ipse autem non respondit eius pro amato nec excusavit eum. Queritur qui maiorem mereretur culpam aut homines obloquentes amato aut amicus tacens non excusans eum.

348. ¶ Contemplava lamich son amat sasubtillava en son enteniment e enamoras en sa volentat e es questio per qual dels dos asubtillava pus fortment sa remembrança a remembrar son amat

Amicus contemplans amatum suum subtilis efficiebatur in intellectu suo et philocaptus erat in voluntate sua. Queritur que duarum potentiarum subtiliorem efficiebat memoriam ad recolendum amatum suum.

344. The Lover lost a jewel that he loved very much. He became depressed, until his Beloved asked him a question: "Lover, which would be more profitable to you, the jewel you used to have or patience with the acts of your Beloved?"[204]

345. The Lover slept, thinking about the travail and obstacles that he faced in serving his Beloved. He became afraid that his works would fail because of those obstacles. But the Beloved sent him conscience, and this awakened him to merit and to the powers of his Beloved.[205]

346. The Lover had to travel on long, hard, and rough roads. The time came for him to set out on them, carrying the heavy load that love makes its Lovers bear. The Lover lightened his soul of worldly cares and pleasures, so his body could carry its load more easily and so his soul could walk those roads in the company of his Beloved.

347. One day some people criticized the Beloved in front of the Lover, but the Lover did not object or defend his Beloved. So the question arises: who was more at fault, the people who criticized the Beloved or the Lover who kept silent without defending his Beloved?

348. The Lover contemplated his Beloved: this sharpened his Intellect and filled his Will with love. So the question arises: which of these most sharpened his Memory for remembering his Beloved?[206]

---

204 A very acute illustration of the distinction between material treasure and spiritual riches. Llull's concern for this issue perhaps reflects contemporary debates over religious poverty, especially the polemics raised by the Spiritual Franciscans. Llull evidently met some of the Spiritual leaders at times during his career.

205 That is, facing obstacles earns merit in the eyes of Beloved, whose power can help the Lover overcome any obstacle.

206 As usual, Llull's question poses a dilemma: the operations of the Intellect and Will contribute equally to the Memory's recollection of God. Llull typically insists on this co-equal operation of the mind's three faculties.

349. ¶ Ab frevor e temor anava lamich en son viatge honrar son amat frevor lo portava temor lo conservava ¶ dementre quel amich enaxi anava atroba suspirs e plors qui li aportaven saluts de son amat e es questio per qual de tots quatre fo mills asolaçat lamich en son amat

Cum fervore et timore ibat amicus in peregrinatione ad honorandum amatum suum. fervor portabat eum. timor conservabat eum dum autem amicus isto modo iret adinvenit fletus et suspiria que portabant salutes ei ab amato Queritur a quo istorum quattuor sociabatur melius amicus in amato.

350. ¶ Esguardava lamich si mateix per ço que fos mirall on vees son amat e esguardava son amat per ço que li fos mirayll on agues conexença de si meteix e es questio a qual dels dos miralls era son enteniment pus acostat

Speculabatur amicus semetipsum ut ipse foret speculum in quo videret amatum suum ut esset ei speculum in quo haberet sui ipsius cognitionem. Queritur cui istorum speculorum plus adherebat intellectus amici.

351. ¶ tehologia e philosophia medicina e dret encontraren lamich quils demana de noves si havien vist son amat ¶ Tehologia plorava philosophia duptava mediçina e dret salegraven e es questio que signifiquen cascu dels quatre significats al amich qui va cerchar son amat

Theologia. philosophia mediçina et ius. obviaverunt amico qui querebat ab eis dicens. vidistis amatum meum. plorabat theologia. dubitabat philosophia Ius autem et medicina letabantur Queritur quid quodlibet quattuor significatorum significet amico querenti amatum suum.

352. ¶ Angoxos e ploros anava lamich encerchar son amat per vies sensuals e per carreres entellectuals e es questio en qual dels dos camins entra primerament dementre cerchava son amat ni en qual lamat se mostra al amich pus declaradament

Anxius et plorans ibat amicus querendo amatum suum per iter sensuale et per iter intellectuale Queritur per quod duorum itinerum prius ibat amicus dum quereret amatum suum et in quo clarius se demonstravit amatus amico.

353. ¶ Al dia del judici dira lamat que hom triy a una part ço que en aquest mon li ha donat [231r] e a altra part sia triat ço que hom ha donat al mon per ço que sia vist com coralment es estat amat ni quals dels dos dons es pus noble e de major cantitat

In novissimo die dicet amatus segregentur ad partem ea que mihi in mundo data sunt atque videantur ab alia parte que mundo data sunt ut videatur quomodo vero corde dilectus fui. et que duorum munerum nobilius est maiorisque quantitatis.

349. The Lover felt fear and fervor as he went on a journey to honor his Beloved: fervor carried him along and fear guarded him. While the Lover was travelling in this way, he met longing sighs and weeping, who brought him greetings from his Beloved. So the question arises: which of these four best maintained the bond between the Lover and his Beloved?

350. The Lover looked at himself as a mirror for seeing his Beloved. He looked at his Beloved as a mirror for knowing himself. So the question arises: which of the two mirrors was closest to his Intellect?[207]

351. Theology, Philosophy, Medicine, and Law met the Lover. He asked them for news and if they had seen his Beloved. Theology wept, Philosophy doubted, Medicine and Law were glad. So the question arises: what do each of these four mean to the Lover who goes looking for his Beloved?[208]

352. Weeping with anguish, the Lover sought his Beloved along the paths of the Senses and the highways of the Intellect. So the question arises: which road did the Lover take first to find his Beloved, and which was the one where the Beloved revealed Himself most clearly to the Lover?[209]

353. On the Day of Judgement the Beloved will ask all people to place on one side what they have given to Him in this world, and to place on the other side what they have given to the world. This will show how heartily He was Beloved and which of the two gifts was best and biggest.[210]

---

207 Llull often uses this traditional image of the soul as a mirror for knowledge of God.
208 Llull frequently criticizes the academic study of these disciplines as deviations from the true quest for spiritual perfection.
209 Llull regularly denounces the philosphers for relying on material data acquired through the Senses, while his system uses spiritual truths attained intellectually. Unlike the questions in most other paragraphs, which pose dilemmas, this question requires an answer in favor of the Intellect. The questions in paragraphs 353 and 354 likewise invite unambiguous answers.
210 Simple catechetical instruction, perhaps conflating Christ's warnings from Matthew 22.21 and 25.31-46.

354. ¶ Amava la volentat del amich si matexa e lenteniment demana li si[li *deleted*] era pus semblant a son amat en amar si matexa o en amar son amat Com sia cosa que son amat sia pus amant si mateix que nulla altra cosa E per aço es questio segons qual responsio la volentat poch respondre al enteniment pus vertaderament

Diligebat voluntas semetipsam. querebat intellectus ab ea utrum esset similior amato suo diligendo semetipsam quam diligendo amatum suum. vel diligendo amatum suum quam diligendo semetipsam. cum amatus plus diligat semetipsum quam quicquam aliud. Queritur per quam responsionem possit voluntas veracius intellectui respondere.

355. ¶ digues foll qual es la mayor e la pus noble amor que sia en creatura respos aquella qui es una ab lo creador per que per ço cor lo creador no ha en que puscha fer pus noble creatura

Dic fatue qui est nobilior et maior amor qui sit in creatura? Qui respondit. ille qui cum creatore unus est quia creator non habet in quo creare possit creaturam nobiliorem.

356. ¶ Estava lamich .i. dia en oracio e senti que sos hulls no ploraven e per ço que pogues plorar trames sa cogitacio cogitar en diners fembres fills viandes vanagloria e atroba en son enteniment que mes gents an a servidors cascunes de les coses demunt dites que no ha son amat e per aço foren sos hulls en plors e sa anima en tristicia e en dolor

Quadam die consistebat amicus in orationibus et sensiit [195rb] non flere oculos suos. ut autem flere posset misit cogitationes ad cogitandum in pecunia in uxore in filiis in fertilibus epulis in mundanis prosperitatibus. atque in inani gloria. invenitque in intellectu suo quamlibet predictarum rerum plures habere sibi servos quam habeat amatus suus confestim ab oculis eius manaverunt lacrime et in dolore et tristicia conversavit anima eius.

357. ¶ Anava lamich consiros en son amat e atroba en la via grans gents e grans companyes qui li demanaven de noves e lamich per ço cor atrobava plaer en son amat no respos a ço que li demanaven e dix que per ço que nos lunyas de son amat no volia respondre a lurs paraules

Ibat amicus considerans in amato suo et adinvenit in via gentes plurimas magnaque consortia et querebant ab eo nova. amicus autem cum inveniret amenitates et decorem in amato suo non respondit eis quicquam ad ea que querebant sed dixit eis. ne elonger ab amato meo nichil respondeo sermonibus vestris.

358. ¶ Era lamich dintre e defora [231v] cubert damor e anava cerchar son amat dehia li amor on vas amador Respos vaig a mon amat per ço que tu sies mayor

Erat amicus intus et extra coopertus amore et ibat querens amatum suum. Amor dixit ei quo vadis amator Qui respondit vado ad amatum meum ut maior sis.

354. The Will of the Lover loved itself. So the Intellect asked whether it resembled its Beloved more by loving itself or by loving the Beloved, since He loves Himself more than anything else. So the question arises: which would be the truest answer that the Will could give to the Intellect?[211]

355. "Say, fool, what is the greatest and noblest love in any creature?" He answered: "The love that unites it with the creator." "Why?" "Because the creator has nothing else that could make a creature nobler."

356. One day the Lover sat praying and felt that his eyes were no longer weeping. So, in order to weep, he sent his mind to meditate on wealth, women, children, food, and pride.[212] His Intellect found that each of these things has more people serving it than his Beloved does. Then his eyes filled with tears and his soul filled with sadness and pain.

357. The Lover walked along thinking about his Beloved. Along the way he met great crowds of people who asked him for news. Since the Lover found such pleasure and beauty in his Beloved, he ignored their questions. He said: "I prefer not to answer you, in order not to stray from my Beloved."

358. The Lover was covered inside and out with love, and went off to find his Beloved. Love asked him: "Where are you going, Lover?" He answered: "I go to my Beloved, so you will be greater."

---

211 God is indisputably the highest object of the Will's desire. The Intellect's question perhaps represents the misuse of reason, which Llull so often denounces.
212 That is, the worldly goods of fortune, family, comfortable living, and high rank, which so many people pursue more avidly than they do God, the Supreme Good.

359. ¶ Digues foll que es religio Respos nedeetat de pensa e desirar murir per honrar mon amat e renunciar al mon per ço que no haja embargament a contemplar lo e a dir veritat de sos honraments

Dic fatue quid est religio? Qui respondit mentis illese puritas et desiderium moriendi ad honorandum amatum meum et renunciatio mundi ut non inveniatur impedimentum ad contemplandum amatum meum et ad dicendum veritatem de honoribus eius.

360. ¶ Digues foll que son treballs plants suspirs plors tribulacions perills en amic Respos plaer damat per que per ço quen sia mes amat e lamich mes guaardonat

Dic fatue que sunt labores. planctus. suspiria fletus tribulationes et pericula in amico? Respondit amicus. placita amati. et quare placita amati? ad hoc ut plus diligatur et ut amico sint maiora premia.

361. ¶ Demanaren al amich amor en qual era major o en lamich qui vivia o en lamich qui muria respos que en lamich qui muria per que per ço cor no pot esser major en amich qui mor per amor e pot o esser en amich qui viu per amor

Interrogaverunt quidam amicum dicentes. in quo maior amor est aut in amico qui vivit aut in amico qui moritur? Respondit amicus. in amico qui moritur. Et quare hoc. respondit. maior amor nequit esse in amico qui amore moritur. maior tamen esse potest amico qui vivit amore.

362. ¶ Encontrarense dos amichs la .i. mostrava son amat e laltre lentenia e era questio qual damdos era pus prop a son amat E per la solucio lamich havia conexença de la demostraçio de trinitat

Obviaverunt sibi duo amici. unus eorum ostendebat amatum alter vero intelligebat eum. Queritur quis eorum esset amato suo propinquior. [esset *deleted*] per solutionem huius questionis cognoscebat amicus demonstrationem divine trinitatis.

363. ¶ digues foll per que parles tan subtilment respos per ço que sia occasio a exalçar enteniment a les noblees de mon amat e per que per mes homens sia honrat amat e servit

Dic fatue quare tam subtiliter loqueris. Qui respondit ut sit occasio ad exaltandum intellectum in nobilitates amati mei et ut a pluribus hominibus magnificetur et diligatur.

364. ¶ Embriagavas lamich de vi qui membrava entenia e amava lamat aquel vi amerava lamat ab sos plors e ab les lagremes de son amich

Inebriebatur amicus vino recolente intelligente et diligente amatum cum fletibus et lacrimis amici sui.

359. "Say, fool, what is religion?" He answered: "Pure thoughts, longing to die for the honor of my Beloved, and rejecting the world so there will be no obstacle to contemplating Him or to speaking the truth about His excellence."

360. "Say, fool, what are travails, laments, longing sighs, weeping, tribulations, and danger to the Lover?" He answered: "Pleasure to the Beloved." "Why pleasure to the Beloved?" "Because thanks to them He is more Beloved, and the Lover earns a greater reward."

361. They asked the Lover: "Is love greatest in the Lover who lived or in the Lover who died?" He answered: "In the Lover who died." "Why?" "Because it can be no greater in the Lover who dies for love,[213] but it can be so in the Lover who lives for love."

362. Two Lovers met: one revealed his Beloved and the other understood Him. So the question arose: which of the two was closest to his Beloved? From the answer the Lover learned about proving the divine Trinity.[214]

363. "Say, fool, why do you speak so obscurely?" He answered: "To provide an opportunity for the Intellect to rise up to the excellence of my Beloved and so that more people will honor, love, and serve Him."

364. The Lover became drunk with the wine of remembering, understanding, and loving his Beloved. But the Beloved watered the wine with His weeping and with tears from the Lover.[215]

---

213 A paraphrase of Christ's commandment in John 15.13.
214 The answer perhaps is that neither was closer, just as one Person of the Trinity is not closer to the others. The revealing and the understanding perhaps symbolize the active and the contemplative lives of devotion, which Llull's own career combined.
215 This image is intriguing for its coincidence with the theme of inebriation from the ecstatic or "drunken" school of sufism, although it seems more obviously to echo the comparison of love to wine and references to the "wine of the Beloved" in the Song of Songs (1.2, 4.10, 7.9, 8.2).

365. ¶ Amor scalfava e aflamava lamich en membrança de son amat e lamat lo refredava ab lagremes e plors e ab hubli[232r]dament dels delits daquest mon e ab renunciament dels vans honraments e crexien les amors com lamic membrava per qui sostenia langors triublacions ni los homens mundans per qui sostenien treballs persecucions

Calefaciebat amor et inflammabat amicum in memoria amati sui. Amatus autem refrigerabat eum lacrimis et fletibus et oblivionibus deliciarum mundi cum renunciatione inanium honorum Itaque augmentabantur amores dum amicus recordabatur quare tribulationes et langores sustinebat et quare mundani homines tribulationibus et persecutionibus affligebantur.

366. ¶ Digues foll que es aquest mon Respos preso dels amadors servidors de mon amat E quils met en preso Respos consciencia amor temor renunciament contricçio companyia davol gent e es treball sens guardo on es puniment

Dic fatue quis est iste mundus. Respondit amicus carcer amatoribus et servis amati mei. Quis incarcerat eos? Respondit amicus. conscientia. amor. renuntiatio. turba iniquorum. et labores sine premio ubi homines puniuntur.

¶ Cor blanquerna havia a tractar del libre de la art de contemplacio per aço volch finir lo libre de lamic el amat lo qual es acabat a gloria e a lausor de nostre senyor deus

Quoniam blaquerna tractaturus erat de libro artis contemplationis voluit ideo terminare hunc librum amici et amati. qui explicit ad laudem et gloriam domini dei nostri qui vivit et regnat in seccula secculorum. AMEN.

365. Love warmed and inflamed the Lover with memories of his Beloved. The Beloved cooled him with tears and weeping, forgetting worldly pleasures, and rejecting worthless honors. So love grew as the Lover remembered why he suffered anguish and tribulation, and why worldly people suffered travail and persecution.

366. "Say, fool, what is this world?" He answered: "A prison for Lovers serving my Beloved." "Who puts them in prison?" He answered: "Conscience, love, fear, renunciation, contrition, and the company of sinners. It is travail without reward, where people are punished."[216]

Since Blanquerna had to work on the book of *The Art of Contemplation*,[217] he finished the *Book of the Lover and the Beloved*, which ends here to the glory and praise of Our Lord God, who lives and reigns forever and ever. Amen.

---

216 Llull evidently conflates traditional devotional conceptions of the world as captivity for the soul with courtly love imagery of the prison of love.

217 This work follows the *Book of the Lover and the Beloved* as a second appendix to the *Book of Blanquerna*.